Bonsai

BY THE EDITORS OF SUNSET BOOKS AND SUNSET MAGAZINE

*Autumn turns foliage of Ulmus parvifolia 'Seiju' into
confetti-like golden display.*

Sunset Publishing Corporation ■ **Menlo Park, California**

Leafless Acer buergeranum (trident maple) shows carefully trained yet naturalistic structure.

Research & Text
Philip Edinger

Coordinating Editor
Sarah Teter Hudson

Design
Nina S. Bookbinder

Photography
Saxon Holt

Additional photography: **Dick Dunmire:** *14;* **Derek Fell:** *91 top;* **Michael S. Thompson:** *15, 17 bottom, 31 top;* **John Trager:** *92 middle*

Small Worlds

Outside of its Asian homelands, bonsai has progressed, in less than a century of time, from a little-understood curiosity to a widely enjoyed art form. It is arguably the most popular horticultural endeavor today; and for every person who is involved with bonsai, there are at least two others who appreciate it as observers.

The reasons for such widespread popularity are not hard to understand. Bonsai presents an outlet for artistic expression and a chance to practice horticultural skills; it is available to anyone with the barest scrap of outdoor space; and it offers the opportunity for camaraderie with legions of enthusiasts.

The generosity of such enthusiasts—beginning with those who contributed to the two previous editions of this book—is reflected in the information contained in these pages. For their sharing of valuable advice and carefully tended bonsai specimens as we produced this edition, we extend our gratitude to Mas Imazumi, Ted King, Dorothy Hayden Land, Janet Price, Bill Sullivan, and Jack Weeks. Our thanks go to the latter two for reviewing the final manuscript.

We are also grateful to bonsai aficionado Barbara Braasch for her copy editing of the manuscript, and to Phyllis Elving for her editorial assistance.

Cover: *A triumph of art and horticulture is this Yeddo spruce (Picea jezoensis) trained in Root over Rock style (see page 31). Bonsai by Mas Imazumi. Cover design by Susan Bryant. Photography by Saxon Holt.*

Editor, Sunset Books: Elizabeth L. Hogan

First printing May 1994

ONTENTS

An Ancient Art

DEFINING BONSAI & TRACING ITS ROOTS

A centuries-old tradition in China and Japan, bonsai fuses the aesthetics of fine art with the skills of horticulture. What originated as an exotic Asian art form has captured the fancy of cultures far beyond its homeland, for bonsai is more than simply evidence of the gardener's ability to copy nature. To many, it represents the very essence of the natural world. In these pages, you'll enter the unique world of bonsai—discovering its cultural significance, encountering its diversity, and learning the fundamentals of its practice.

Stalwart Cedrus atlantica (Atlas cedar) recalls venerable forest sentinels, belies careful training that accounts for well-displayed structure, precise branch placement.

WHAT IS BONSAI?

Defined simply, a bonsai is a dwarfed plant growing in a container. In fact, the term "bonsai" combines two Japanese words that provide the most basic definition of this living art form. "Bon" is a tray or pot, while "sai" means to plant.

Basic definitions, though, may not truly describe an object. Strictly speaking, after all, a painting may be merely a smattering of pigments applied to taut cloth or some other flat surface. A symphony might be described as an assortment of tones represented by abstract shapes arranged on horizontal lines and presented by a group of people interacting with various inanimate objects.

These examples suggest just how inadequate it is to simply call a bonsai a "plant in a pot." The components may be described, but the essence of the art form is missing.

A PHILOSOPHICAL STATEMENT

It's easy to assume that by putting a small plant in an even smaller container we have created a bonsai. One may even see bonsai as little more than dwarfed, even deformed, curiosities which, if only left in the wild or planted in the garden, would have the chance to grow to their intended sizes and shapes.

But to fully understand bonsai and what it expresses, we need to extend our outlook beyond the traditional Western viewpoint. Basic to this understanding is a realization of how differently Eastern and Western cultures regard the earth and its elements.

Looking at the natural world

In traditional Eastern thought, humans are one part of the natural world, no different from—or superior to—a rock, a tree, or a bird. Western culture, on the other hand, has traditionally seen *Homo sapiens* as the highest achievement of evolution on the planet, with the ability, if not the mandate, to control nature. This fundamental philosophical difference in Eastern and Western thought can be summed up as "coexistence" versus "dominance."

Thus, a Westerner may regard that small potted plant as simply a personal possession. But in Asian cultures it may instead be seen as a manifestation of the natural world's life force and accorded the respect due to an equal.

Intricate branching, sturdy trunk of bonsai Ulmus parvifolia 'Seiju' (corkbark elm) suggest full-sized tree.

Wild specimen of Quercus lobata (valley oak) shows a natural model for bonsai design.

The essence of bonsai

A bonsai, as nature in microcosm, is created to evoke the *spirit* of nature, and frequently it suggests a particular aspect of the natural world, such as a windswept cliff, a craggy mountaintop, or a forest glade. When you view a bonsai, you see an abstraction of nature and respond to it.

Because bonsai specimens are intended to be evocative statements rather than photographically accurate reproductions, they have an artistic kinship with Western culture's impressionist school of painting. Impressionist painters use brushwork to suggest rather than to depict. The result draws the viewer into the picture and stimulates the imagination to interact with it.

A fine example of bonsai has the same effect. The sweep of a branch may suggest a seaside cliff with waves crashing below. The deliberately weathered branches of a gnarled juniper may evoke the thin mountain air at timberline.

EVOLUTION OF AN ART

The art of bonsai is inextricably linked to Japan. Bonsai was introduced to the Western world from that country, and much of the terminology we use in the practice of bonsai is

Weatherbeaten beauty of this Juniperus californica (California juniper) capsulizes the essence of high mountain terrain where harsh conditions reign supreme.

tual refreshment. Inevitably, potted plants became a part of this gardening endeavor—and from potted plants stemmed bonsai.

The first evidence of bonsai as an art form is shown in painting. Chinese frescoes dating back sometime before A.D. 220 clearly show floral bonsai—what we would think of as flower arrangements—in complementary containers. Painted during the late Han Dynasty, these frescoes were discovered in the 1970s. The first depiction of bonsai plants, rather than flowers, comes from Tang Dynasty tomb murals dating from A.D. 760.

The word "bonsai," rendered in two Chinese characters, appeared sometime around A.D. 400. Furthermore, the text that contained the word made reference to the practice of bonsai as existing before the start of the Eastern Chin Dynasty in A.D. 317.

The practice of bonsai increased in popularity and diversity during subsequent Chinese dynasties. Different schools of bonsai art evolved, based on particular philosophical ideals, artistic precepts, and regional attitudes. Individual plant specimens, similar to those we see today, became one form of expression. Another was the pictorial "landscape bonsai," in which dwarfed plants were combined in shallow trays with rocks to represent mountains, water to depict lakes and rivers, and miniature structures to lend scale.

From China to Japan

Considering the early cultural exchange that linked China and Japan, it was inevitable that bonsai would reach the attention of the Japanese. And given the Japanese appreciation of nature and sensitivity toward beauty, it's not surprising that bonsai exerted a special appeal for them.

Initial contact between China and Japan came in about 200 B.C., but it was not until considerably later, during the time of the Tang Dynasty (A.D. 618–906), that Japanese emissaries traveled to China expressly to study Chinese culture. This cultural delegation was certainly exposed to bonsai, virtually assuring its transmission to Japan.

Japanese. However, the first record of bonsai actually comes not from Japan but from China.

Chinese beginnings

As the most ancient of Asian cultures, China has long been called the "Mother of Gardens." In part, this is due to the vast numbers of native Chinese plants common today in gardens throughout the world. But it also acknowledges the long-standing Chinese tradition of creating gardens—for both temporal pleasure and spiritual refreshment.

Ravages of nature are suggested by the "jinned" apex of this Juniperus californica (California juniper) bonsai.

The first records of bonsai in Japan, like those in China, are pictorial. The earliest occurs in a scroll dating from the year 1185; other notable depictions exist in two works from around 1300. Within the first half of the fourteenth century, bonsai made its appearance in Japanese writing.

Continuing refinement

Chinese bonsai often featured elaborately distorted, even grotesquely deformed, plants. They were quite different from what we think of today as traditional bonsai. For hundreds of years, Japanese practitioners built upon the Chinese styles. But gradually changes occurred as bonsai artists began to seek out wild plants that had been artfully distorted by the elements.

The Japanese aristocracy displayed a fondness for bonsai specimens collected from the wild. Small trees that had been weathered into unusual and sometimes fantastic shapes became highly prized. The acquisition of such naturally dwarfed trees spurred vast collections, and good plants therefore became harder to find. Eventually, it became necessary to replicate nature's handiwork by skillfully training domestic plants.

In the mid-nineteenth century, training methods for creating bonsai specimens were refined by Japanese practitioners. The aesthetic principles of Japanese bonsai as we know them today were codified during this period.

BONSAI TODAY

Because China and Japan were largely closed to Europeans for many centuries, Western contact with Asian culture was at a tantalizing minimum. China allowed trade only through

Like a tree on a steep bank, this Wisteria sinensis (Chinese wisteria) flings its branches into open air.

Popularity of bonsai has spawned specialized bonsai nurseries where you can find tools and pots, starter plants, even young specimens in the process of being trained.

designated ports. Japan was closed to all foreigners except for one Dutch ship each year from 1637 until Commodore Matthew Perry and his U.S. warships forcibly opened its ports in 1854.

As a result of these Chinese and Japanese policies of isolation, the Western world had little contact with bonsai until relatively recent times. In 1901, a lecture on bonsai cultivation presented to members of England's Japan Society failed to elicit general interest. But in 1907, records show, there was a bonsai collection at Windsor Castle. And the public response to bonsai displays at a London exhibition in 1909 was enthusiastic.

The first serious practitioners of bonsai in the United States were Japanese-American residents, who brought their knowledge and appreciation of the art with them when they settled on the West Coast in the early decades of the

twentieth century. But it was U.S. servicemen returning from Japan after World War II who gave bonsai its first widespread exposure in this country.

Today, bonsai societies abound, both on the local and national level, and bonsai magazines and books are plentiful. Experts tour the country giving lectures and demonstrations, and exhibits are common at nurseries, botanical gardens, and museums. Bonsai plants are even featured in retail catalogs.

In less than a century's time, bonsai has become an internationally practiced art, rooted in the Japanese tradition formalized in the nineteenth century. How does one explain the relatively rapid rise of such widespread interest? Perhaps it is simply difficult to resist a pastime that combines art, history, and gardening, at the same time promoting both beauty and a sense of tranquility.

BONSAI SOCIETIES

Bonsai enthusiasts can join numerous orgnizations that deal solely with the art and culture of bonsai. National and international organizations offer exposure to a broad range of experience; local societies reinforce enthusiasm with fellowship and bonsai exhibits.

NATIONAL, INTERNATIONAL ORGANIZATIONS

American Bonsai Society
P. O. Box 358
Keene, NH 03431

Bonsai Clubs International
2636 W. Mission Road, #277
Tallahassee, FL 32304

International Bonsai
P. O. Box 23894
Rochester, NY 14692

REGIONAL SOCIETIES

Bonsai Societies of Florida
Florida Bonsai magazine
579 Man O War Cr.
Cantonment, FL 32533

Golden State Bonsai Federation
Golden Statements magazine
Marie Rohde
6385 Zulmida Avenue
Newark, CA 94560

Puget Sound Bonsai Association
P. O. Box 15437
Seattle, WA 98115

LOCAL SOCIETIES

This listing gives locations of many local bonsai groups. For full information, send $3.50 to the American Bonsai Society (address above) for the Directory of North American Bonsai Societies.

Alabama Birmingham, Decatur/Huntsville, Mobile

Arizona Payson, Phoenix, Tucson

Arkansas Little Rock

California Arcadia, Arcata, Chico, Crescent City, Encino, Gardena, Hanford, La Cañada, Los Angeles, Modesto, Napa, Oakland, Palo Alto, Riverside, Sacramento, San Diego, San Francisco, San Jose, San Mateo, Santa Barbara, Santa Maria, Santa Rosa, Temple City, Vacaville

Colorado Denver

Connecticut New Haven, Newington, Stamford

Florida Boca Raton, Daytona, Fort Lauderdale, Fort Pierce, Miami, Naples, Orlando, Pensacola, Port Charlotte, St. Petersburg, Tallahassee, Tampa, West Palm Beach

Georgia Atlanta

Hawaii Honolulu, Kailua-Kona, Pearl City

Illinois Glencoe, Glen Ellyn, Peoria, Rockford, Rock Island, Sandwich, Springfield

Indiana Evansville, Indianapolis

Iowa Des Moines

Kentucky Louisville

Louisiana Baton Rouge, Lafayette, Lake Charles, New Orleans

Maine Bangor

Maryland Baltimore, Bethesda, Bowie

Massachusetts Danvers, Wellesley

Michigan Ann Arbor, Bay City, Kalamazoo, Pontiac, St. Clair Shores, Traverse City

Minnesota Minneapolis

Missouri Kansas City, St. Louis

Nevada Las Vegas

New Hampshire Keene

New Jersey Westwood

New Mexico Albuquerque

New York Brooklyn, Buffalo, Farmingdale, Fayetteville, Ithaca, Queens, Rochester, Voorheesville, Watertown

North Carolina Morehead City, Raleigh

Ohio Cincinnati, Cleveland, Columbus, Dayton, Newark, Sandusky

Oklahoma Oklahoma City, Tulsa

Oregon Coos Bay, Corvallis, Eugene, Medford, Portland, Port Orford

Pennsylvania Erie, Harrisburg, Kennett Square, Lehigh Valley, Lewisburg, Philadelphia, Pittsburgh, Reading

South Carolina Columbia, Seabrook Island

South Dakota Brookings

Tennessee Nashville

Texas Abilene, Austin, Beaumont, Corpus Christi, Dallas, Fort Worth, San Antonio

Utah Salt Lake City

Vermont Jericho

Virginia Fairfax, Hampton, Lynchburg, Norfolk, Roanoke

Washington Marysville, Olympia, Puyallup, Seattle, Sequim, Tacoma

Wisconsin La Crosse, Madison, Menasha, Milwaukee

Wyoming Laramie

The Design of Bonsai

ARTISTIC PRINCIPLES, BONSAI STYLES

A basic knowledge of plant growth habits and gardening techniques is all that's really needed to train and care for a bonsai. But visualizing just how you want a plant to look—and determining how best to achieve that result—calls for artistry. Creating a bonsai is really an artistic endeavor similar to painting, ceramics, or sculpture. Part of the pleasure of this art form is developing your own artistic sensibility and refining your technique. In this chapter we'll show you the many directions you can take to create bonsai.

Carefully tended Informal Upright–style Juniperus californica (California juniper) appears to have mostly dead wood of "jin" and "shari"; only a tuft of foliage betrays life.

A DESIGN FROM NATURE

When studying the art and practice of bonsai, there's no need to be intimidated by what may at first appear to be a host of inflexible rules. You'll find that there are many approaches to achieving artistically satisfying results in bonsai.

It's not necessary to learn about all the different bonsai styles or even to memorize all the information on a single style before you begin working with a bonsai plant. Your project will evolve over time. As with any type of art, the novice improves with experience—and so does the artwork. Nobody expects a beginner to turn out a masterpiece right away.

Remember, too, that the artistic satisfaction of working with bonsai goes hand in hand with the pleasure of gardening. You'll experience the joys of nurturing a living plant and watching it evolve through the seasons—and the years. Though a beautifully trained, mature bonsai is your aim, the process of working toward that goal is what gives the greatest satisfaction.

DESIGN CONSIDERATIONS

Reduced to its most basic description, a bonsai is a plant in a pot. The difference between the bonsai and a nursery plant in a 1-gallon can is simply a matter of design. The nursery plant is watered and fertilized to become a full and husky specimen; the bonsai plant is carefully nurtured and trained to develop artistically according to a preconceived plan. It's this artistic design that creates a bonsai that will evoke the spirit of nature.

Developing an eye

To develop a sense of natural design, take a look at trees growing in the wild. Notice how weather, topography, and soil conditions cause them to grow in a particular manner. The knowledge you gain from your observations will help you replicate nature's handiwork.

You'll notice that trees tend to lean toward water and lowland and away from the wind. And you'll see why a tree will grow with a twisted, leaning, or even prostrate trunk in one place but staunchly upright in another.

Note that a tree's foliage grows where it gets maximum sunlight. Trees that cluster in tight groves bear most of their leaves at the top of the shared canopy. These trees grow straight and tall, their branches often reaching upward rather than outward. On the other hand, trees

Great age (more than 100 years) has not dimmed the vigor of this Kurume azalea (Rhododendron hybrid).

that are not crowded together tend to spread their branches more widely and bear a full canopy of foliage.

An eye on bonsai. A careful study of well-trained bonsai illustrates how these principles of natural shaping can be translated into a small plant in a pot.

Bonsai exhibits offer good opportunities for three-dimensional views of plants and close-ups of trunks, branches, and foliage. And bonsai societies often sponsor demonstrations of training and pruning in conjunction with shows. These bonsai shows offer a chance to glean practical advice from other enthusiasts. For information on bonsai organizations, turn to page 11.

Photographs of bonsai, including the ones in this book, are another good resource. Many publications contain pictures of outstanding specimens that can provide both inspiration and design guidance.

The appearance of age

When you look at bonsai, you'll notice something beyond the obvious fact that these plants are small. Except for young bonsai-in-training, most specimens seem much older than their diminutive size suggests. And they may also appear to be veterans of years of struggle against natural forces that have significantly altered their forms. Indeed, in some carefully tended specimens the flame of life may appear to be barely flickering.

While it's true that you'll see bonsai specimens older than you are (in exceptional cases, even older than several generations of your family), not all good bonsai plants are old. Actual age is of less importance in bonsai than the illusion of age.

Some plants may actually have lived for years in the wild before being collected and nurtured as bonsai (see pages 46–47). But many specimens that appear to be ancient are really works of art—products of the human hand working with nature to produce the *appearance* of age. This carefully designed look is an integral part of the various bonsai styles presented on pages 24–37.

Creating the appearance of age by cutting and peeling bark from a bonsai is a special technique discussed on pages 74–75.

Artistic unity

All parts of a bonsai—roots, trunk, branches, and foliage—must be included in the overall design plan if your specimen is to appear unified. And the artistic concepts of balance, proportion, line, and form must all be taken into consideration to create this unity. When these elements are harmoniously integrated within a bonsai, the appearance of maturity is

In Slanting style, this Larix laricina (American larch) is a good example of overall unified design.

Informal Upright–style Picea jezoensis (Yeddo spruce) shows balanced placement of branches and foliage.

convincing. If they are ignored, you are likely to produce a specimen that is uninspiring at best, or even grotesque.

Balance & proportion. The location of branches and foliage, the variety in branch sizes, and the placement of the plant in the container all contribute to creating pleasing balance and proportion.

Balance doesn't dictate symmetry: you'll seldom find a perfectly symmetrical bonsai. Instead, balance refers to distribution—a heavy branch on one side balanced by a curve on the other, for example.

Proportion refers to the relative sizes of a plant's elements. If, for instance, a branch on

one side is too massive for its counterbalance, it will seem out of proportion.

Line & form. The "line" of a bonsai composition is determined by the relationship of the plant's apex to the trunk base. Does the highest point lie in a vertical line directly above the base or in a diagonal line to it?

Traditional bonsai design is based on the "rule of three": the lowest point symbolizes earth, the midpoint represents man, and the highest point signifies heaven. These three points form an asymmetrical triangle. A bonsai's lowest and farthest-reaching branch tip is considered the lowest point of this triangle, the apex of the plant is the highest point, and the foliage extremity on the side opposite the lowest point is the midpoint.

APPLYING DESIGN PRINCIPLES

Good design can't be expressed in a set of absolute rules. If it could, all bonsai would look much alike. But there are some general artistic principles to consider in creating an aesthetically pleasing bonsai. These principles cover all parts of the plant—trunk, branches, foliage, and roots—as well as the direction from which you view it (called "plant aspect") and the container in which it is growing.

Trunk

Though no one part of a bonsai is more important than another, the structure of its trunk is central to its style. A thick trunk suggests a mature tree, whether or not it is actually old, but a trunk that is *too* thick simply appears to be out of proportion. A workable rule of thumb is that the height of the bonsai should be roughly six times the width of the trunk's base.

The trunk should taper gracefully and naturally to its terminal point. A cylindrical trunk (same thickness at the top and bottom) makes the bonsai look out of proportion. For this reason, you shouldn't lop off a trunk to create an apex at a suitable height without then training the uppermost branch into vertical position

Thick, rugged trunk of Ulmus parvifolia 'Hokkaido' suggests a tree of great age.

have relatively few branches, and those are carefully spaced and directed. The branching pattern establishes the basic outline of the bonsai and shows the trunk to best advantage.

Branches should vary in size and length. Spaces between branches also should vary, gradually diminishing toward the plant's apex. You might think that having the lowest branch long, the one above it shorter, and the next one shorter still would create the desired effect. Except for some Formal Upright styles, however, such a rigid gradation produces an overly stiff, artificial effect.

As a general rule, the combined length of the two longest branches (usually the lowest ones) should equal about half the height of the bonsai. But there are exceptions. If, for

Continued on page 20

to continue the trunk's line and taper. Broom style (page 33) is the one exception to the rule.

With few exceptions (see Coiled and Twisted styles, page 28), trunk curves should be kept to a minimum. Depending on the style you are trying to achieve, one or two gentle bends may be pleasing, but too many are distracting and may appear artificial. In most cases, you should avoid abrupt bends. And a good bonsai never features a curve that arches toward the front of the plant.

A trunk that appears aged, even weatherbeaten, is cherished. But a trunk that is scarred from wiring or bad pruning is never admired. As a bonsai matures, its trunk will look more venerable. To add to the appearance of age, refer to pages 74–75 for creating *jin* and *shari*.

Branches

A bonsai's natural look is actually the result of carefully arranging and training its branches. Left to their own devices, trees often branch heavily and randomly. Most bonsai, in contrast,

Carefully trained Pinus contorta (shore pine) shows a precise arrangement of branches in decreasing lengths.

CONTAINER CHOICES

The container you choose must be a harmonious part of the complete bonsai, as important as any element of the plant it contains. While elaborately decorated pots were in vogue earlier in bonsai history, today's emphasis is on the total composition. The successful container is one you hardly notice. Three elements are important: surface finish, shape, and orientation.

Surface finish. Glazed pots are good for flowering and fruiting plants; their glazes can be chosen to complement the flowers and fruit. Glazed containers can be used for deciduous plants in general, but be sure to coordinate the glaze with foliage color, using lighter shades for light foliage and darker colors for dark, rich leaves. To use a glazed pot with evergreens, choose a dark color with no ornamentation.

Unglazed containers are widely used. You will find them in a variety of soft, dark colors, including brown, red-brown, dull purple, and gray. The unobtrusive colors and finishes are particularly pleasing with evergreens.

Shape & depth. To create a harmonious composition, consider the relationship between plant style and container shape. You'll find pot recommendations for each of the bonsai styles

Glazed bonsai containers come in a wide range of surface treatments, shapes, and sizes. The tiny decorated pot features Nandina domestica (heavenly bamboo).

presented on pages 24–37. Generally, it's best to plant fairly upright bonsai in rectangular and oval pots, positioning the trunk off-center.

Pot depth usually should equal the thickness of the base of the trunk or the thickest trunk in a group. The length of the container should be about two-thirds the height of an individual plant or about one-third the height of the tallest tree in a grouping.

Cascade, Literati, and Windswept bonsai look good planted in round, square, or hexagonal pots. To provide stability as well as artistic balance, their containers traditionally have been at least as deep as they are wide. Nowadays, these styles are also potted in fairly shallow containers and displayed atop decorative stands.

Orientation. Every plant or group planting has a front side (see page 21), so it is important to coordinate that with the configuration of the container. In general, shallow rectangular and oval containers should present their long side to the front; square pots should show a straight side rather than a corner. Deep containers may offer either a straight side or a corner to the front. A deep hexagonal container always presents an angle to the front.

The subtle tones and unobtrusive surface of unglazed pottery are suitable for virtually all bonsai styles and plants. Decorative touches consist of surface design in bas-relief.

Fruiting bonsai, such as this yellow Malus (crabapple), produce normal-size fruits despite reduced plant size.

The shape of individual branches is important, although that will vary according to the style of the bonsai and the particular plant. Viewed from above, a branch together with its side branches should generally have a wider spread near the trunk and taper toward a point at the tip, forming an outline in a diamond, triangle, or arrowhead shape. From the side, a branch should present a narrow profile, with side branches growing in the same plane as the parent limb. And, to maintain proper proportion, branches should be noticeably smaller in diameter than the trunk.

When you shop for suitable bonsai plants, don't expect to find specimens that meet all of these branch criteria. Look for as many positive characteristics as you can find, but view plants with an eye toward pruning and training to eliminate defects and enhance the effect you desire. A young plant with branches that tangle together, cross in front of the trunk, or grow too profusely in one direction may just be an ugly duckling awaiting a swanlike transformation at your hands.

Foliage

A bonsai's leaves should both reveal and complement the trunk and branch structure. Too thick a leaf canopy obscures the structure; too sparse a coverage gives the appearance of an unhealthy plant—and may in fact indicate just such a condition.

Foliage also should be in proportion to plant size. To a limited extent, you can reduce leaf size through leaf cutting (see page 64); but you shouldn't use this as a permanent remedy for overlarge foliage. For best results, choose smaller-leafed plants for training. Some of the best bonsai subjects are profiled in "Plants for Bonsai," beginning on page 83.

Though you can control foliage size somewhat, no amount of pruning will reduce the size of any flowers or fruits a bonsai plant bears. A flowering cherry or quince bonsai, for example, will display full-size blossoms annually, and fruiting plants such as crabapples may produce normal-size fruits. The effect of this momentary disproportion can be anywhere from startling to

. . . Continued from page 17

instance, you have a short plant with a thick trunk, the combined length of the bonsai's two longest branches might actually be greater than its height.

In many of the most pleasing specimens, the angle of slope is roughly the same for all branches. The branches of many needle-leafed evergreens, however, provide an exception. In nature, the branches of these trees may point upward when young but angle downward when old. Effective bonsai of these plants may reflect this natural inclination.

amusing. Such a discrepancy in proportion is a fault technically, but it's a guaranteed conversation piece.

Roots

An example of the importance of carefully exposing roots in some bonsai styles is shown on pages 36–37. However, the appearance of roots, or even the *suggestion* of them, is important in all bonsai.

You should be able to see clearly the point where a trunk starts to fan out into the root system. In many specimens, it is desirable to reveal the tops of large roots as they extend out from the trunk's base and down into the soil.

Artistic judgment governs the placement of roots as well as branches. When conspicuous, roots should spread out in all directions from the trunk. They should vary in size and spacing, not look like spokes in a wheel. If there is an especially large and protruding root, it should be at the back of the plant.

Aspect: *front & back*

In nature, a tree can't be said to have a front or a back; it all depends on where the viewer stands. A bonsai is a three-dimensional work of art that is meant to be appreciated from a particular vantage point, however, so the issue of front or back is important. The photos on page 22 illustrate this point.

When selecting a potential bonsai, and certainly when you begin training a plant, your first consideration will be to determine its front. The front should be the side with the greatest potential for displaying the structure of the plant to best advantage. It should be relatively open, with no large branches growing directly toward the viewer. There should be no large forward-protruding root, nor should any curves in the trunk bulge out toward the front. When you view a finished bonsai, only the apex should incline forward slightly.

The back of a bonsai contributes depth to the composition. While branches that extend toward the front are undesirable, branches that

Exposed roots of this Rhododendron (azalea) show desirable spacing and radial pattern around trunk.

grow toward the back of the plant are essential, because they add a third dimension. They also create a backdrop of branches and foliage against which the the bonsai's forward structure is displayed.

Though the back of the plant will not be viewed directly, it should still be well arranged —not simply a mass of twigs and leaves. Awkwardly placed, ill-proportioned branches that might detract from the front view should be removed.

Rarely will you find young nursery plants with perfect fronts. Almost all will need some pruning and training (see pages 63–72) to present their best faces. Examine a plant from all angles to see if there is a viewpoint that is free of undesirable features. If not, look for an angle that may possess only a single flaw that could be remedied by training or pruning.

Containers

A bonsai isn't a plant in just any pot. The container you use is part of the total artistic composition. Turn to pages 18–19 for photographic examples and a discussion of containers suitable for bonsai.

Front view of Windswept–style Juniperus horizontalis (creeping juniper) clearly shows plant structure.

Back view of same plant shows much more foliage, forming backdrop for front-view structural detail.

BONSAI CLASSIFICATION

Bonsai is an art of endless variety: each specimen is an individual. Nonetheless, all plants can be classified in two ways: by their size and by their basic design style.

SIZE

Finished bonsai can range all the way from a few inches to over 4 feet in height. Today, you may find bonsai separated into just two categories; *shohin* for plants up to 10 inches high, and *bonsai* for specimens 10 inches to 4 feet tall. Historically, though, size has been subdivided into five categories:

Miniature . . . . **under 6 inches**
Small . . . . **6 to 12 inches**
Medium . . . . . **12 to 24 inches**
Large . . . .**24 to 36 inches**
Extra-large . . . **36 to 60 inches**

The most commonly grown specimens fall within the small and medium sizes. It's more difficult to simulate age in good proportion in miniature bonsai, and the sheer bulk of large specimens makes them cumbersome.

STYLE

The many shapes you find in bonsai are actually variations on basic well-defined styles. When you look beyond the differences between various specimens, you will begin to notice a number of general themes.

Many of these broad bonsai style categories are defined by *trunk formation*—whether the trunk is straight, curved, slanted, or twisted. The majority of these trunk-based styles feature plants with a single trunk. The *character of branches* determines other styles. Still other

Extra-large and miniature, they're both bonsai. Burly Quercus agrifolia (coast live oak) shelters tiny plant of Serissa foetida trained in similar fashion.

styles are based on *root configuration* or on a total *composition* of a number of elements.

A gallery of the best-known bonsai styles is presented in the following 14 pages. These styles are grouped according to their common stylistic denominators, and each is identified by a descriptive name in English as well as its identifying Japanese term.

Formal Upright Sequoia sempervirens (coast redwood).

The shape, aspect, or inclination of a bonsai's single trunk determines whether it falls within this category. These seven individual Single-Trunk styles include some of bonsai's most familiar designs as well as some of the most diametrically opposed—from the absolutely vertical Formal Upright to the dramatically down-sweeping Cascade.

UPRIGHT

The bonsai practitioner distinguishes between two Upright styles: Formal and Informal. The shape of the trunk establishes the distinction.

Formal Upright (chokkan)

Picture a plant with a perfectly straight, virtually cylindrical trunk that tapers gradually as it rises vertically from the soil, and you are likely visualizing a Formal Upright. The trunk base splays outward just enough to indicate that radiating roots give good support. An example in nature is the majestic tree that stands alone in a field or lawn.

The lowest and longest branch should appear about a third of the way up the trunk, extend to one side of the trunk, and perhaps angle slightly toward the front of the plant. The next branch as you proceed upward should be a bit smaller and extend toward the opposite side of the bonsai, angling slightly forward. The third branch will be smaller yet, extending toward the back of the plant.

This ascending spiral pattern repeats as you progress up the trunk to the apex, the branches getting smaller and more closely spaced as they approach the top. A finished Formal Upright specimen will be nearly cone-shaped.

Ordinarily, large branches that point toward the front of a plant are undesirable because they obscure the structure rather than enhance it, but small branches in the upper third of the plant may project forward slightly if they fit the overall design pattern. To determine which branches to keep, remember that branches on opposite sides of the trunk should not be at the same level, and no branch should be directly above another one.

Plants. Any tree that naturally grows straight and tall is a good candidate for Upright training. Particularly good specimens include *Celtis* (hackberry), *Fagus* (beech), *Juniperus* (juniper), *Larix* (larch), *Liquidambar styraciflua* (sweet gum), *Picea* (spruce), *Pinus* (pine), *Sequoia sempervirens* (coast redwood), and *Sequoiadendron giganteum* (giant sequoia).

Containers. For plants designed to convey a sense of majesty, you want to provide a sound

Informal Upright Pinus thunbergiana (Japanese black pine).

footing. Formal Upright styles look best in rectangular and oval containers. Choose containers that will be deep enough to prevent plants from looking top-heavy.

Informal Upright (moyogi)

As the name suggests, the Informal Upright looks like a slightly relaxed Formal Upright. The trunk may display a slight curve, a bit of a slant, or both; many good specimens have trunks shaped like an elongated letter "S." The plant's tip is nonetheless in a direct line over the base, giving a sense of stability despite the less rigid trunk. For anyone just starting to train bonsai, this is the easiest style to work with, since plants with slightly sinuous trunks are fairly common.

In training an Informal Upright plant, follow the general spacing guidelines outlined for Formal Upright. Also take note of two points about trunk bends: avoid a curve that projects

Slanting Pinus thunbergiana (Japanese black pine).

toward the front of the plant; and be sure that the branches extend from the outside of a trunk's curve, not the inside.

Plants & containers. Follow the guidelines suggested for Formal Upright plants.

SLANTING (SHAKAN)

The Slanting bonsai style abandons the sense of stability you find in the stalwart Formal Upright and the asymmetrical but centered Informal Upright styles. Slanting-style plants perform balletlike balancing acts. With trunk angles of 30° to 45° from vertical, they suggest the possibility of toppling. Only the branch arrangement and the apparent strength of the roots indicate that gravity might not win.

Roots, in fact, are as important as branches in the composition. Strong surface roots should be evident, especially on the side away from the slant. Their thickness and sinewy nature should imply a firm grip on the soil as a counterbalance to the inclined trunk and far-flung limbs. On the side of the slant, exposed roots should appear as a buttresslike hump.

General branch placement follows the guidelines for the Formal Upright style, with the lowest and largest branch extending away from the slant. Overall, the greater concentration of weight should be on the side away from the slant even though the greater branch reach can be in the direction of the slant. This differs from the near-perfect radial symmetry of the Formal Upright style.

The branches of the Slanting style should be arranged in horizontal layers that are parallel to the ground or bend slightly down.

Plants. Each of these plants adapts well to the Slanting style: *Acer palmatum* (Japanese maple), *Celtis sinensis* (Chinese hackberry), *Juniperus* (juniper), *Larix* (larch), *Picea* (spruce), and *Pinus* (pine).

Containers. Oval and rectangular containers are pleasing bases for bonsai in the Slanting style. You can use a more shallow container than you would with an Upright style to underscore the sense of delicate balance.

Literati Picea jezoensis (Yeddo spruce).

Literati (bunjingi)

Ancient Chinese scholars and artists known as "literati"—learned ones—painted mountain landscapes that depicted picturesquely gaunt trees whose angled trunks and sparse branches bespoke a struggle for space and sunlight. The Literati style of bonsai recalls those venerable survivors, evoking images of a countryside in which spectacular scenery and harsh conditions manage to coexist.

The branches of plants in this style are few, short, irregularly placed, and spaced primarily in the upper third portion of the trunk. In some Literati plants, the trunks lean at angles similar to those of the Slanting style; but these trunks, unlike those of Slanting bonsai, will bend or twist tortuously as though the plants had been forced to compete with others to reach light. Other Literati specimens more closely follow a trunk pattern of the Informal Upright style. In either case, sparse branches growing near the top of the plant are what most clearly define it as Literati.

The lack of specific guidelines for branch placement and trunk aspect makes it important for the trainer to have a good artistic sense. Well-executed specimens display an almost fragile elegance.

Plants. The following plants will give the appropriate sparse appearance: *Casuarina equisetifolia* (horsetail tree), *Juniperus* (juniper), *Larix* (larch), and *Pinus* (pine).

Containers. To complete the impression of austerity, choose a simple, inconspicuous container. A shallow round or slightly irregular pot of unglazed clay will be suitably unobtrusive.

Cascade (kengai)

While most trees stand more or less upright, a Cascade bonsai appears to completely succumb to gravity. Only a few inches of trunk grow upward before it starts to arch over the edge of a container and flow downward.

A Cascade style takes its design from nature's "mountain goat" trees. These tenacious specimens cling with the barest of rootholds to steep slopes and cliff faces and are then forced downward by landslides, snowslides, and their uncertain grasp on scant soil. But, while the trunks grow down, the branch ends turn up, often resulting in a series of foliage plateaus. So this style always gives the appearance of a plant trying to right itself.

Cascade bonsai are separated into two divisions. The trunk and branches of a *Full Cascade* plant extend below the base of the container. If the branches fail to reach the pot's base, the plant is instead a *Semicascade (han-kengai)* bonsai. Depending on the depth of the pot, a Semicascade may be either nearly horizontal or pendent.

In both Cascade and Semicascade bonsai, the branches closest to the roots are the largest; subsequent branches diminish in size as they

Cascade Cedrus atlantica 'Glauca' (blue Atlas cedar).

Containers. Choose a fairly deep pot—Cascade plants need the counterweight of soil to keep from toppling over, and their branches simply look better cascading over a deep pot. Round and hexagonal containers are most frequently used, but square pots are also appropriate. In square and hexagonal containers, the trunk of the bonsai should arch over a juncture of two sides.

COILED (BANKAN)

Occasionally you will encounter bonsai in the Coiled style, featuring an irregularly twisted trunk ascending in a broad coil. Frequently the trunk will grow at a slant from the soil level, starting to coil close to the container. Well-placed roots radiate from the trunk base. If the plant has a slanted trunk, the roots should be more prominent on the side opposite the slant. Branches are fairly short, appearing in the upper portion of the plant and projecting out in all directions.

Plants. This style calls for flexible plants that are not inclined to produce long branches. *Juniperus* (juniper) and *Pinus thunbergiana* (Japanese black pine) are good choices.

Containers. Plant Coiled bonsai in oval or rectangular pots of shallow to moderate depth.

TWISTED (NEJIKAN)

Like a barber-pole spiral, the trunk of the Twisted bonsai winds its way upward—sometimes looking as though two trunks are wrapped around one another. Trees growing at timberline are often distorted this way and may even exhibit significant portions of dead trunk. Therefore, Twisted bonsai often feature *shari* (see page 75) to emphasize the spiral. Trunk shape and branch placement generally follow the same principles used for Informal Upright plants.

Plants & containers. The plants and containers specified for Coiled bonsai also work well for the Twisted style.

approach the tip of the trunk. Despite a Cascade plant's downward growth, many specimens feature an apex branch that grows upward from the back side of the trunk just before the trunk begins its downward arch.

Plants. Many plants can be encouraged to cascade. Some of the best are *Camellia sasanqua* (Sasanqua), *Cedrus* (cedar), some species of *Cotoneaster* (cotoneaster), *Juniperus* (juniper), *Pinus thunbergiana* (Japanese black pine), and *Pyracantha* (firethorn).

COMPOSITION STYLES

Group Planting, Acer palmatum (Japanese maple).

These distinct style categories appear to have nothing in common. What relates them—and makes them different from other styles—is that the total effect depends on more than a single plant's character. Rather, it is the result of a careful composition of more than one plant in a single container, or of plants arranged in combination with rocks.

GROUP PLANTINGS (YOSE-UYE)

Also known as Forest Plantings, bonsai in the Group Planting style are composed of individual plants with separate root systems. Most Group Plantings contain odd numbers of plants. You'll need at least five trees to give the effect of a forest. To make a Group Planting using just two trees, follow the design guidelines on page 35 for Double Trunk bonsai.

In Group Plantings, the total effect is more important than the beauty of the individual trees. You can even use plants that have defects a bit too pronounced to stand alone. One tree in the group should be larger than the others to serve as a focal point, and no two trees should be exactly the same size.

Group Planting, Picea glauca 'Conica'
(dwarf Alberta spruce).

For the best effect, don't place the trees at uniform distances from one another. Instead, space them irregularly in several clusters. Position the tallest tree to one side of the center of the pot, then place the next in size just to the opposite side of center. The finished planting outline should approximate an asymmetrical triangle.

Perspective is the key to good Group Plantings. Placing the largest trees in the foreground creates the sense of the forest receding from you; planting the largest trees in the background reverses the effect.

If your container is large enough, you can even compose two separate but overlapping Forest Plantings. In such compositions, the complete Group Planting as well as each of its parts should be in the shape of an asymmetrical triangle.

Plants. Good choices are plants that normally grow in groves or forests. Use the same kind of tree for your whole forest, or at least similar trees with similar habits and needs. Any of the following will make effective Group Plantings: *Acer* (maple), *Celtis sinensis* (Chinese hackberry), *Cryptomeria japonica* (Japanese cryptomeria), *Larix* (larch), *Liquidambar styraciflua* (sweet gum), *Picea glauca* 'Conica' (dwarf Alberta spruce), *Pinus thunbergiana* (Japanese black pine), *Sequoia sempervirens* (coast redwood), and *Taxodium distichum* (bald cypress).

Containers. Long, shallow containers are best for Group Plantings. They may be oval, rectangular, or even irregular in shape.

ROCK PLANTINGS

Rocks form a conspicuous part of the bonsai composition in two different styles. Their English names clearly describe them.

Clinging to Rock (ishitsuki)

In this style, the plant grows entirely on a rock. The rock becomes the plant's real container; the pot underneath it serves simply as a base to the composition.

Clinging to Rock Juniperus chinensis procumbens 'Nana'.

The Clinging to Rock style is essentially a landscape in the Chinese tradition. The rock represents a mountain, and the plants portray trees clinging to its rugged slopes.

Craggy rocks are best to use for this style because their crevices can hold a little soil. After you attach one or more small plants to the rock you have selected (see pages 54–55 for directions), you place the finished composition in a shallow container, usually filling it with water or fine sand.

There are no strict rules for training plants in the Clinging to Rock style. The objective is simply to make the planting look natural.

Plants. For an effective design unity, choose plants with small leaves for Clinging to Rock bonsai. Common selections include some *Cotoneaster* (cotoneaster), *Juniperus* (juniper), *Picea* (spruce), and small-needle *Pinus* (pine).

Containers. Very shallow oval, rectangular, and round containers form good bases for Clinging to Rock compositions. The best shape to use depends on the individual rock you use as your "container."

Root over Rock (sekjoju)

To visualize the Root over Rock style, think of draping the roots of an Exposed Root plant (described on page 37) over a sturdy rock. The objective is to have roots tenaciously clasping a rock as though they had naturally clung to its surface from infancy. But in contrast to the Clinging to Rock style, the Root over Rock plant will extend its roots into the soil that supports the rock.

Guidelines for training Root over Rock bonsai are presented on page 55.

Plants & containers. The suggestions on page 37 for Exposed Root plants and containers also apply to Root over Rock bonsai.

Root over Rock Pinus thunbergiana (Japanese black pine).

BRANCH STYLES

Broom Zelkova serrata (sawleaf zelkova).

Though these utterly distinct styles all feature single-trunk plants, they are not classified according to how the trunk grows. Instead, they are grouped by the way the branches grow.

BROOM (HOKIDACHI)

Hold a broom with the head pointing up and you have a clear picture of this style. The trunk should be straight and upright, with numerous slender branches that create a delicate interlacing pattern within a mushroom- or gumdrop-shaped outline. All main branches should originate from close to the top of the trunk.

In contrast to most other styles, Broom plants need a large number of branches and twigs to create the desired effect. With an appropriate plant for this style, you can cut the trunk to the height you want, then encourage branches from just beneath the cut.

Plants. Choose deciduous trees that tend to grow naturally in the desired shape. Two good choices are *Ulmus parvifolia* (Chinese elm) and *Zelkova serrata* (sawleaf zelkova).

Containers. Broom bonsai look best in shallow oval and rectangular containers.

WINDSWEPT (FUKINAGASHI)

It takes little imagination to visualize a Windswept bonsai. Its branches all point in one direction from a slanting trunk, as though the plant had been shaped by prevailing winds.

The trunk angle and root formation of the Windswept style recall the Slanting style (page 26). Branches are generally larger near the base of the plant, decreasing in size as they ascend the trunk. But regular spacing and arrangement are not the criteria for this style; your goal is to create the appearance of survival under adversity.

Because wind-battered trees frequently contain dead branches and scarred trunks, Windswept bonsai are good subjects for *jin* and *shari* (see pages 74–75).

Windswept Juniperus horizontalis (creeping juniper).

Plants. The diverse choices include *Buxus* (boxwood), *Casuarina equisetifolia* (horsetail tree), *Juniperus* (juniper), *Olea europaea* (olive), *Pinus* (pine), and *Quercus* (oak).

Containers. Windswept specimens usually appear in round or rectangular containers.

WEEPING (SHIDARE-ZUKURI)

Take an Informal Upright or Slanting trunk, adorn it with pendent branches, and you have a Weeping bonsai. Branching occurs in the upper third of the trunk, with the weeping limbs hanging down directly from the trunk or from short side branches. Many Weeping bonsai specimens branch in all directions from the trunk; others are entirely one-sided.

Plants. Your only choices are naturally weeping trees such as *Fagus sylvatica* 'Pendula' (weeping European beech), *Prunus subhirtella* 'Pendula' (weeping cherry), *Pyrus salicifolia* 'Pendula' (weeping willow-leafed pear), and various *Salix* species (weeping willow).

Containers. Fairly shallow oval and rectangular containers are appropriate.

MULTI-TRUNK STYLES

Double Trunk Ulmus parvifolia 'Seiju'—with Cascade Cotoneaster horizontalis (rock cotoneaster).

As the name suggests, Multiple-Trunk bonsai are grouped by how many trunks they have. The trunks originate from one root system, rising from the soil or an enlarged plant base. Select a plant with two or more stems growing from ground level; cut out any you don't need.

DOUBLE TRUNK (SOKAN)

Both trunks in a Double Trunk bonsai clearly rise from the same root system, but one is larger, taller, and more dominant. That trunk should bear the more substantial branches.

The two trunks form a fairly narrow "V" at the base and rise generally upright but not parallel to one another. If they curve, it should be in the same direction. Branches should be spaced much like those of Formal and Informal Upright bonsai. The branches of the two trunks should not grow into each other, but the trunks and their branches should form one cohesive unit with an almost cone-shaped outline.

Plants. Choose plants that naturally tend to branch from ground level or will send up multiple sprouts if cut close to the ground, such as *Alnus* (alder); *Celtis sinensis* (Chinese hackberry); *Chaenomeles* (flowering quince); *Crataegus* (hawthorn); *Ilex* (holly); *Juniperus* (juniper); *Malus* (crabapple); *Olea* (olive); *Picea* (spruce), especially *P. jezoensis; Pinus* (pine), especially *P. parviflora;* and *Quercus* (oak).

Containers. Fairly shallow oval and rectangular pots are compatible with this style.

TRIPLE TRUNK (SANKAN) & FIVE TRUNK (GOKAN)

The trunks of Triple and Five Trunk bonsai should vary in height, with the tallest being the most massive. The tallest trunk of a Triple Trunk often appears in the center with a lower trunk positioned on either side.

Branch placement is similar to that for Double Trunk style. Regardless of the number of trunks, the composition should always look like a single plant.

Plants & containers. Follow the suggestions for Double Trunk bonsai.

CLUMP (KABUDACHI)

The Clump style features a tight cluster of trunks. The sole difference from the Five Trunk style is that there are more trunks.

Plants & containers. Follow the suggestions for Double Trunk bonsai.

Five Trunk Pinus thunbergiana (Japanese black pine).

ROOT STYLES

Exposed Root Zelkova serrata (sawleaf zelkova).

At first glance, you might not see any common points among these styles. Their distinctive root formations, however, unite them in one broad style category.

EXPOSED ROOT (NE-AGARI)

A plant on stilts is an accurate capsule description of the Exposed Root style. In nature you may find such trees near water, growing along a stream that floods and exposes their roots.

Creating this style of bonsai is simple, but it takes several years to develop roots that will tolerate full exposure. Your first training task is to direct root growth downward in a constricted space. And the first step is to remove the soil from around the roots and repot the plant in a deep, narrow container.

You can make a suitable training pot by removing the top from a 1-quart or ½-gallon milk carton to create a bottomless, deep and narrow container. Nestle the base of the training pot into a broader container of potting soil, then plant your specimen in the training pot.

In time, the plant's roots will grow down into the soil of the lower container. After a year of such training, unpot the plant during its dormant period to check root growth. If the roots have grown into the lower pot, cut off the top part of the training pot and remove soil to expose the upper portion of the roots.

When the root system in the lower container appears to be sturdy enough to support the trunk and branches of your bonsai, pot the plant in a bonsai container with the constricted roots exposed.

There is no set style for trunk shape and branch placement of Exposed Root bonsai, but avoid incongruous effects. You wouldn't expect to see a Formal Upright tree atop a perch of bare roots. Trunk and branch patterns modeled after Slanting, Semicascade, Windswept, or even Weeping styles will look more natural.

Plants. You can train any plant that shows an inclination toward dramatic growth. Avoid bolt upright trees such as *Sequoia sempervirens* and *Sequoiadendron giganteum* (redwoods) and *Metasequoia glyptostroboides* (dawn redwood).

Containers. You'll find Exposed Root bonsai growing in square, round, irregular, oval, and rectangular containers.

RAFT (IKADABUKI) & CONNECTED ROOT (NETSUNAGARI)

One of nature's clear manifestations of the will to live is the tree that falls, yet remains alive to become several trees. Nourished by the root system of a downed trunk, some limbs grow upright in a small, linear grove. The Raft style copies nature's example. See page 54 for instructions on creating a Raft planting.

The similar Connected Root style features several trunks growing from a single root that lies on the soil surface or just beneath it. The trees may form a curving or sinuous grove.

Plants. For Raft training, *Juniperus* (juniper) is an easy subject. Other good plants include *Acer* (maple), *Carpinus* (hornbeam), *Cryptomeria japonica* (Japanese cryptomeria), *Liquidambar styraciflua* (sweet gum), and *Pinus* (pine).

Plants for Connected Root bonsai include *Alnus* (alder), *Chaenomeles* (flowering quince), and *Liquidambar styraciflua* (sweet gum).

Containers. Raft and Connected Root bonsai are best in shallow oval and rectangular pots.

Raft planting, Juniperus horizontalis (creeping juniper).

*O*ff to a Good Start

CHOOSING & POTTING PLANTS FOR BONSAI

When you see an established bonsai, it's difficult to imagine this mature plant as a formless youngster. Yet all bonsai specimens started as humble seeds or cuttings that had to be carefully trained in order to become the artfully formed plants you see today. In the following 16 pages, you'll learn the practical points that lead to this transformation: how to start or select a good bonsai candidate, how to prepare the proper soil for your bonsai, and how to plant the specimens you have chosen.

Nursery display shows assorted suitable bonsai plants ready for potting and training.

OBTAINING PLANTS FOR BONSAI

While almost any tree or shrub could be trained as a bonsai, not all plants will turn into good bonsai specimens regardless of your best efforts. The photograph below illustrates this point. It's important, therefore, to take care in your selection of plants for bonsai training. For a look at some proven candidates, turn to the encyclopedia of bonsai plants on pages 83–95.

You can approach the creation of bonsai in either of two ways: by training a plant in a particular desired style or by letting a plant's individual characteristics dictate the way you train it. If you know what style you want to develop—Literati, Cascade, or Raft, for instance—you can select plants that lend themselves to training in that style. Whether you begin with seeds, cuttings, or purchased seedlings, you'll more easily be able to achieve your goal if you start with the right plants.

But suppose you wander through a nursery and spot a larger, container-grown plant that appears to be a good choice for bonsai treatment. In that case, you would assess the plant's potential and start training it into the style its form naturally suggests.

STARTING FROM SCRATCH

To the dedicated gardener, nothing is more satisfying than starting your own plants. The most basic approach is to begin with seeds. Taking cuttings, layering, and grafting are methods of creating new plants from existing ones.

Select plants with good structure and small leaves, such as Serissa foetida, Pinus thunbergiana, Cotoneaster 'Lowfast', and Juniperus procumbens (foreground), also Kurume azalea (left rear). Avoid large-leafed plants such as trio in back.

Bonsai from seed

Nothing seems closer to magic than raising plants from seed. And aside from the personal satisfaction of watching a green sprout appear from a seemingly lifeless speck, raising your own seedlings gives you the chance to grow rare or unusual plants. Mail-order companies offer seeds of potentially good bonsai plants that seldom appear in nurseries.

Time is the one drawback. Typically, it takes 4 to 6 months between planting seeds and the appearance of seedlings. Then the seedlings need time to grow to a satisfactory size for bonsai training. This may mean 2 years for fast-growing trees and shrubs and as long as 5 years for slower-growing plants.

To experiment with raising bonsai plants from seed, select trees and shrubs that germinate easily and grow fairly rapidly. Some good choices include most *Acer* species (maples), *Aesculus* (buckeye), *Fraxinus* (ash), *Liquidambar* (sweet gum), and *Zelkova*.

The essentials. To start your seeds, you need a well-drained soil free of organisms that can attack seeds or seedlings. You can buy a standard commercial potting mix at a nursery or garden center, or you can make your own. A time-honored formula combines equal parts peat moss and builder's or river sand.

Start seeds in clean containers. You can use clay or plastic pots, plastic flats, or kitchen discards—aluminum pans, foam and plastic cups, and cut-down milk cartons—as long as you punch drainage holes in their bases.

Starting your seeds. In nature, seeds are shed in summer or autumn and covered with the barest layer of soil and leaves until they germinate in late winter or early spring. Optimum conditions for germination vary widely among plants, but try to duplicate nature's timetable as closely as you can. Generally, plants native to cold-winter regions need some winter chilling before they will sprout; plants from mild-winter regions germinate without significant chilling.

If you're not concerned about how many seeds germinate, the easiest approach is to simply sow them in containers and leave them out-

Both seeds and seed-starting containers come in a variety of sizes and shapes. Large seed is Aesculus (buckeye).

doors until they sprout, watering as needed to keep the soil moist but not soggy. (Soggy soil encourages destructive organisms.) In regions with cold winters, you'll need to put the containers in a cold frame (see page 81) or surround them with soil or organic material such as leaves, sawdust, or compost. Pots directly exposed to the air may get too cold. If you are growing mild-climate or subtropical plants in a cold climate, keep containers in a cool greenhouse or other sheltered location.

To achieve the best possible rate of germination when you are sprouting seeds of cold-winter natives in a mild-winter region, chill seeds in your refrigerator before sowing them. Put them in a sealed plastic bag or shallow plastic container with a mixture of equal parts moist peat moss and sand, then place in the vegetable crisper section of the refrigerator.

How much chilling time seeds require varies, depending on the plant. If you have no specific information for a particular plant, chill seeds about 60 days. Some seeds will germinate during the chilling period; check frequently, and plant any that have sprouted. After the chilling period, plant all unsprouted seeds.

Once seeds germinate, make sure they get plenty of light, but protect them from excessive heat. Water just enough to keep the soil moist.

Bonsai from cuttings

Except for pines and a few other conifers, most bonsai plants can be started from cuttings. There are two advantages to this technique. You know you will get just the same kind of plant that furnished the cutting (not always true with seeds), and you get a training-sized plant much sooner than you would from seed.

Cuttings fall into three categories, depending on the age of the wood. Some trees and shrubs can be rooted all three ways; others grow best from just one or two types of cuttings. The plant encyclopedia beginning on page 83 indicates the preferred cutting method for each kind of plant.

■ *Softwood (or tip) cuttings* come from new spring and summer growth. They are the succulent ends of stems that are flexible but will break when bent sharply enough. These cuttings root quickly, but they need a moist atmosphere around stems and leaves to keep them from wilting and dying while they root. (See the photo at left.)

■ *Semihardwood cuttings* come from newly matured growth in summer and early autumn, after stems have finished lengthening. The stem should be firm enough to snap when bent sharply. If it simply bends, it's too old. Both needle- and broad-leafed evergreens usually grow successfully from semihardwood cuttings.

■ *Hardwood cuttings* come from mature stems formed during the past growing season. Many deciduous plants root easily from hardwood cuttings taken after leaves drop in autumn or early winter.

Making your cuttings. Use sharp pruning shears to take cuttings. Make softwood and semihardwood cuttings about 6 inches long, hardwood cuttings 6 to 9 inches. For the cutting's base, cut straight across the stem, just below a leaf or growth bud; remove leaves from lower half of cutting. Hardwood cuttings (and some semihardwood cuttings) are taken from the center portion of a branch; make the top cut on a slant just above a leaf or growth bud.

Some plants root better from a "heel cutting." This is a stem cut or pulled off so that it includes a small portion of the parent branch. Trim the heel with a sharp knife so that its edges and cut surface are smooth.

Dip the bottom end of each cutting in a rooting hormone, then insert it in a fast-draining rooting medium such as the potting soil recommended for seeds on page 41. When

A potpourri of cuttings shows softwood cuttings potted and enclosed in plastic bag to retain moisture. Hardwood cuttings can be started in containers, as shown, or planted in the open ground. Small jar holds rooting hormone.

you see new growth, chances are your cutting has taken root. When cuttings seem to be growing well, move them into individual pots.

Bonsai from layering

Two layering methods will root stems without removing them from the parent plant. The success rate is high because the layered plant continues to receive nourishment from the parent root system while it develops its own roots.

■ *Ground layering* works best with shrubs that branch close to the ground. A supple, low-growing stem is partially buried in the soil beneath the plant. Roots then form on the buried portion of the stem, creating a new plant.

■ *Air layering* involves bringing rooting medium up to the stem. Select a healthy stem, girdle it by cutting away a ring of bark (as wide as the branch diameter), then surround this section with moist material, such as sphagnum moss, overwrapped in plastic. Roots will form from the wounded bark region. If you layer a stem that already has branches above the layer, you may create a small specimen ready for bonsai training.

It may take 4 to 6 months (for some air-layered plants) or as long as a year (for ground-layered plants) before new growth appears on the layered section. At that time you can sever the "new" plant from its parent and move it to its own container.

Bonsai from grafting

Grafting bridges the gap between starting plants from seeds or cuttings and creating bonsai from already-growing specimens. Grafting isn't particularly difficult, but it does take a bit of dexterity that is only developed by practice.

Grafting involves joining a growing root system of one plant (called the "stock") with what is essentially a cutting (known as the "scion") from the plant you desire. When a graft is successful, the scion becomes a new plant supported by the root system of the stock.

For a graft to succeed, the cambium layer (the tissue between bark and heartwood or

For ground layering, nick bark of branch near ground level where you want roots to form, dust cut with rooting hormone, then bury stem (held in place by a rock) in shallow trench so that the leafy branch end points upward.

For air layering, cut ring of bark from pencil-thick stem. Dust exposed area with rooting hormone, surround with moist sphagnum moss secured by string, then wrap with polyethylene plastic secured with electrician's tape.

For grafting, first cut pencil-thick scion from plant you want to propagate; trim cut end into tapered wedge.

Next, make slanting cut just above soil level into trunk of stock plant selected to furnish roots.

Insert wedge-trimmed stem into slanting cut so that cambium layers (just inside bark) come into contact.

Finally, wrap graft with plastic grafting tape to ensure contact. In time, top growth of stock should be removed.

pith) of stock and scion must unite. This requires clean cutting, fast and agile work, and some special tools and materials. The photographs on this page show a procedure known as veneer grafting, one of the easiest grafting methods for the beginner to tackle.

Despite the greater difficulty in starting plants by grafting than by other methods, there are good reasons for doing so. Grafting lets you propagate plants that are difficult to root from cuttings and hard to grow from seeds. And if you have a rare plant, or a plant that will not bear seeds for a number of years and won't grow from cuttings (such as many pines), grafting lets you start a new plant immediately.

Usually grafting is done between two plants of the same genus—pine to pine, maple to maple, and so forth—but there are exceptions. Many of these are plants in the rose family—apples, crabapples, cherries, plums, and quinces, for example—which may succeed with rootstock of one kind and scion of another.

A grafted plant often betrays its origin by a visible graft union, the point at which stock and scion fuse. The graft union may be somewhat more enlarged than the stem above and below, or it may simply show as a ridgelike scar. In some cases, you can spot a graft union by a change in bark character.

An obtrusive graft union is a fault when it comes to judging a bonsai's quality. The less noticeable the union the better.

STARTING WITH PLANTS

Though it's satisfying to start your own bonsai plants, it can also be rewarding to shop for them at a nursery. You have the challenge of hunting for specimens that have training potential and the joy of finding just the plants you want. Best of all, these plants may be ready for immediate training.

Some nurseries carry small specimens labeled "bonsai plants" at fairly modest prices. Sold in 2- to 4-inch pots, some will have just a single stem and tuft of foliage, while others may show the beginnings of branch structure.

But plants suitable for bonsai come in all sizes, even though they may not be labeled as bonsai material. Look among 1- to 5-gallon container stock for specimens that appear healthy and vigorous but not too tall or spindly. Try to find plants with thick, strong trunks. Evaluate the shape and arrangement of major branches to see if the plant's basic form suggests a particular style of training.

Rotate the plant to determine which side would be its front. Consider whether you would need to remove certain branches, bend the trunk, or wire the structure to accentuate a particular form. Don't limit your search to perfect specimens—even imperfect nursery plants can be made into fine bonsai.

You might easily overlook these plants, but sparse specimens of Juniperus horizontalis, Acer palmatum, and Viburnum tinus offer good bonsai potential.

BONSAI FROM THE WILD

It's possible to find plants growing in the wild that might become good bonsai specimens. Depending on a plant's size, however, it may take several years before you can view it as bonsai. And you'll need to temper your collecting zeal with caution—digging and removing plants from private and most government-owned property without permission is illegal. But rural homeowners may find a number of young plants in their own yards, and even suburbanites may discover volunteer seedlings for use as starter plants.

When to dig

Digging a plant in its dormant period (autumn to spring for deciduous plants) minimizes shock during the transplant operation. If you must dig a deciduous plant during the summer, spray it first with an antitranspirant (sold at nurseries) or remove about half of its leaves to keep moisture loss to a minimum.

Weathered Juniperus californica (California juniper) growing in transition container before bonsai potting.

Evergreen plants, both broad- and needle-leafed types, are generally most dormant from winter to early spring. The best time to dig them is shortly before they're ready to put out new growth. Though the risk is greater, you can also dig them after the new growth has firmed up, from late summer to early autumn.

Collection tips

If you're foraging for seedlings in your yard, all you'll need is a small shovel and a few 1- and 2-gallon containers. Dig leafy plants with root balls intact, and temporarily pot them right away to keep the roots moist. Deciduous plants collected during their dormant season can be dug bare root, but be sure to keep their roots moist until you can pot them.

If you go farther afield, a few additional tools are useful. A lightweight, collapsible army or camping *shovel* is convenient to carry. A small *pry bar* is optional but handy for prying roots from rocks or stony soil. Sharp *pruning shears* are a must for cutting back roots and branches; a small *pruning saw* will handle cuts too large for shears. Carry a *container of water* to moisten leaves, roots, and packing material; use a *spray bottle* for leaves.

Any time you dig a sizeable plant in full leaf, you need *wrapping for root balls* to keep them intact until replanted. You can use burlap or polyethylene plastic sheeting secured with twine, or simply encase the root ball with chicken wire.

Digging

For any sizeable plant with foliage, start by clearing all debris and other growth from beneath the plant. Prune out any unnecessary branches. To outline your dig, trace a circle on the ground around the plant about one-third the plant's height in diameter. For short, spreading plants, draw the circle at the tips of the branch spread.

Dig a trench just outside the circle, cutting any roots you encounter. When the trench is about as deep as the circle's diameter, surround it securely with chicken wire to hold the soil together. Secure the cut wire ends by wrapping them together or threading them together with a length of wire.

Free the plant by carefully digging under the root ball from all sides. Gently tilt the root ball, slide more wire beneath it, and lift the plant. Wrap the root ball in moist burlap or plastic sheeting to retain moisture.

Moisten the foliage with a spray of water, and keep it moist to prevent wilting. To keep the plant from dehydrating, place it out of direct sunlight and away from wind. Move it gently to keep the root ball intact.

Planting & training

At home, plant the specimen as quickly as possible. Most collectors prefer potting the plant in a container just slightly deeper and broader than the root ball. Shelter the plant from wind and direct sun, and water just enough to keep the soil moist but not soggy. Moisten the foliage daily, more frequently in hot weather.

The new roots of winter and spring transplants should be sufficiently developed after several months so that you can place plants where they'll get sunshine. You can also begin liquid fertilizing (see page 60). You won't need to moisten foliage as frequently until the weather gets warmer. Postpone fertilizing for summer and autumn transplants until the next spring.

Large specimens need at least a year, longer if there is little new growth, before they are disturbed again. The sign of a successful transplant is the start of healthy new growth—

Ancient Quercus agrifolia (coast live oak); in the wild, lower part of trunks was buried.

indicating that the plant is also producing new roots. When your transplant has made a good transition, you can repot it in late winter in a container that is deeper than the ultimate bonsai pot, but more shallow than the first container in which it was planted.

Remove the plant from its pot and cut back the larger roots by as much as half their length to reduce the size of the root ball. If there are a large number of new roots around the edges of the root ball, trim them back by about a third. Then repot the plant in the shallower container.

Do a bit of branch pruning to compensate for root loss. Don't prune too drastically; just cut back young growth that isn't essential to the basic shape. Give the plant the normal after-transplant care described on page 52.

If the plant grows well during the ensuing year, you can take it out of the pot the following winter. Trim the roots and the new top growth, and consider moving it into a bonsai container. From then on, simply follow the routine regimen of care and training outlined on pages 58–73.

𝒫LANTING PROCEDURES

Anyone who has grown potted plants will be familiar with the basics of planting. But beyond the basics, you'll find particular techniques and principles that apply just to the art of bonsai.

The exact procedures of planting also depend on the size of the plant you are potting. If you're just starting to train a nursery plant taken from a 3- to 5-gallon container, you'll need to give it an interim period in a container that is slightly smaller and more shallow than the one in which it has been growing, but not as shallow as its final bonsai pot. Give the plant a year in this container to adjust to its reduced root system and smaller confines. Then you can unpot it, prune the roots again as described on page 50, and plant it in a bonsai container.

If you're starting with a small nursery specimen or are repotting a bonsai-in-training, you can move it directly into a bonsai container, following the planting advice on pages 50–52.

INITIAL STEPS

Before you can pot a plant, you need to do some advance work. Have potting soil on hand, prepare the container you will use, and ready your plant for potting.

Preparing the soil

Like most plants grown in containers, a bonsai needs soil that drains freely but still retains moisture. As water moves down through soil, it initially fills all of the spaces between soil particles. But surface evaporation and uptake from plant roots reduce the amount of water in the soil and let in air—an interchange that is vital to plant health. When water takes up most of the space between soil particles, it doesn't leave room for air; over time, the roots virtually drown. In soil that retains too little moisture, on the other hand, the roots have enough air but will die from lack of water.

Sandy soil, composed primarily of large mineral particles, allows free passage of water; this soil is called "well drained." The much smaller and flattened particles that produce clay soil let water percolate down very slowly; such soil is known as "poorly drained." Therefore, for the perfect potting soil you want to combine the free drainage offered by sand with some of the water retention of clay.

The key to creating a good soil is organic matter, the decaying remains of plants and animals most familiar to gardeners in the forms of peat moss, wood byproducts, animal manures, and compost. When added to soil, organic mat-

Secure screen over pot's drainage hole with a copper wire "staple." Bend wire into a "U" shape, then make a circular twist at each corner; push ends through screen and bend them back against bottom of pot.

Nursery plant of Juniperus conferta (shore juniper) ready to be started on the road to becoming a bonsai.

ter lodges between particles and particle aggregates, absorbing some of the water that passes through.

A *soil formula*. It has been said that there are as many formulas for bonsai potting soil as there are enthusiasts. Some nurseries sell packaged potting soil for bonsai. But you can make your own general purpose bonsai potting soil by blending equal parts packaged potting mix or compost, builder's or river sand, and good garden soil. Run the mixture through a window screen and discard the fine particles that go through; then use ¼-inch mesh screen to remove lumps and rocks from the remaining soil.

While most deciduous plants and broad-leafed evergreens will do well with this mixture, many needle-leafed and coniferous evergreens need a grittier, faster-draining soil. For these plants, combine 2 parts sand, 1 part potting mix or compost, and 1 part good garden soil.

Preparing the container

If you are going to plant in a used container, first clean it thoroughly with hot water and a brush to remove any old soil. Swab the inside of the container with a 50 percent solution of chlorine bleach and water to eliminate any organisms that could cause plant disease, then rinse thoroughly.

If you are planning to use a new unglazed clay container, or one that has not been used for some time, soak it in water for about an hour prior to planting. This will keep the pot's porous clay from pulling moisture out of the potting soil.

All containers need one or more drainage holes. To prevent potting soil from washing away through these holes, the standard bonsai technique is to cover them with pieces of window screen or hardware cloth held in place by wires, as illustrated in the photo on the facing page. To anchor a plant's root ball (necessary for all but the smallest plants), also bring a U-shaped length of wire up through the drainage hole (or holes) and screen. If there is but one drainage hole, slip a small peg or dowel through the bottom of the "U" on the container's underside; this will keep the wire from being pulled through the drainage hole.

Preparing the plant

The first step in potting is to remove the plant from its existing container. With a chopstick,

Begin plant preparation by carefully removing soil from plant roots; then untangle roots and stretch them out.

With sharp shears, cut back roots, removing about two-thirds of the length; spray with water to keep moist.

loosen the roots from the confines of their root ball, teasing roots apart and removing soil in the process. When they're sufficiently loosened, use your fingers to gently untangle roots and stretch them out.

It's important to keep the roots moist at all times during the potting process in order to prevent transplant shock. Keep a spray bottle of water at hand, frequently misting roots with water as you work.

Pruning the roots. The aim of root pruning is to eliminate a portion of the older, thicker roots in order to encourage the growth of new feeder roots. The thick roots primarily anchor the plant; feeder roots supply it with water and nutrients necessary for growth.

Young plants from small pots may need no root pruning, or just a trim of long roots, to fit into their bonsai containers. Larger specimens will need about two-thirds of their length and at least a third of the total root mass removed. The idea is to cut from the bottom and sides of the root mass, flattening it out on the bottom and rounding the sides while decreasing the diameter. If there is a taproot (a main root growing al-

most vertically downward), cut it back completely. Spray the roots frequently with water to keep them moist.

As you cut the root mass, be sure to leave a fairly symmetrical pattern of roots radiating outward from the trunk. If your design calls for exposing any large roots at the base of the trunk, be careful not to cut or scar them. The spread of the pruned root mass should extend to about two-thirds of the surface area of the container. The depth of the root mass should be about a third to half the depth of the container.

PLANTING

Now you're ready to put your plant in the container. If you are planting a bonsai-in-training in an interim pot, simply treat it as you would any container plant. Positioning of the plant in the pot is not critical, as this will not be its final container.

If you are planting a specimen directly into its bonsai pot, however, positioning and careful attention to bonsai planting procedures are of prime importance.

Finished pruning leaves shallow root mass, rounded sides; plant is ready for potting in bonsai container.

Start by spreading a thin layer of gravel in the bottom of the prepared bonsai container. Then cover the gravel with 1 inch of prepared bonsai potting soil, and proceed through the following steps.

Positioning your plants

Before you position a plant in its bonsai pot, have a clear picture in your mind of how you want it to look. The goal is visual balance, not a symmetrical planting. Here are some general guidelines.

■ *In a rectangular or oval container*, place the plant off-center. Position it so that its base is about a third of the way from one end of the container and just to one side of an imaginary end-to-end center line.

■ *If you're planting in a round, square, or hexagonal container*, center the plant. One exception to this rule is the Cascade style of bonsai (see page 27), in which the trunk is positioned slightly off-center.

■ *When planting a grove of trees*, arrange them so that they fall within an irregular triangle, no side of which aligns with a side of the container. Place the largest tree off-center and roughly a third of the container's length from the nearest edge.

Water the finished planting to make good soil contact with roots; use watering can with fine-spray nozzle.

Partially fill container with potting soil, position the plant, then use chopstick to work in more soil around roots.

Settling in the roots. Once you have positioned a plant in the bonsai pot, settle its root mass into the potting soil, holding the plant in place with one hand. (Now is the time to draw anchoring wires up through the drainage hole and wrap them over the root ball, working the ends unobtrusively back into the soil.) With your other hand, add more soil to the container, working it around the roots with your fingers. When the plant is steady, use a chopstick to thoroughly work the soil in and around roots.

When planting a grove of trees, work the soil into the root system of one tree before planting the next. If trees will grow close together, you may be able to hold several with one hand while you add soil with the other.

Once the plant is firmly settled and the soil is well worked into the root system, you're ready to add the rest of the soil. The top of the main soil mass should fall about ¼ inch below the rim of the container.

Before you add the remaining soil, check plant placement for proper depth. The juncture of roots and trunk or stems should be at most just barely covered with soil when the planting is finished. In many bonsai, the bases of major roots are left exposed to convey a sense of strength and stability.

If a plant is too low in the container, you can raise it by pulling upward while gently rocking it from side to side. When you've determined the plant's proper level, brush away any excess soil, or add more if necessary.

Watering

Watering a newly potted bonsai plant keeps its roots moist and helps settle them solidly into the soil. The simplest method is to use a watering can with a fine-spray nozzle to water the soil surface, continuing until water flows out of the drainage hole.

After watering the newly potted plant, moisten the foliage (if the plant is in leaf) with a fine mist of water from the spray bottle. To help the plant become re-established in its new container, continue moistening foliage on a daily basis for several weeks.

If your tap water is heavily treated with chemical additives such as chlorine or sodium, you will want to water your bonsai with distilled water or collected rainwater. Never water plants with artificially softened water.

Initial care

Pruning and transplanting are a shock to a plant, so care after potting is important.

Put the plant in a protected area for about a month, sheltering it from drying winds, excessive heat, direct sunlight, and pelting rain. Water enough to keep the soil moist but not soggy (see page 59 for general watering guidelines). Frequently mist or gently sprinkle the leaves to keep them from drying out. The hotter the weather, the more watering and misting will be required.

Don't fertilize the plant for at least two months following potting.

FINISHING TOUCHES

The simplicity of a bonsai specimen, the soil in which it grows, and the shape of its container work together to make an evocative statement. But some plants may be further enhanced with the addition of moss or rocks.

A mossy carpet

A bit of green carpet beneath a bonsai conveys the impression of a forest. It also helps keep the soil moist and prevents it from washing away when you water. But keep moss from covering a plant's base where it will obscure the juncture with the roots and hold too much moisture against the trunk.

Dried and powdered moss is available at some nurseries. You simply sprinkle the dried moss over moist soil, tamp it firmly into place, and water with a fine spray to create instant moss. To establish a healthy layer of moss, mist the soil frequently or cover it with a sheet of translucent plastic for a few weeks. Keep the bonsai out of direct sunlight until the moss is established.

You may even be able to collect your own moss. Check damp areas of your garden that receive little sunlight. Even the shady sides of garden stones or shaded margins of brick patios may host moss colonies. In the woods, look for moss on the shady sides of moist rocks or re-

A mossy carpet over soil surface suggests a tree in the forest. Keep moss from obscuring roots at trunk base.

Jagged rocks complement plants, such as this pine, that would naturally grow in rugged mountain regions.

taining walls or on soil near stream banks. Collect the velvety moss that grows on soil or stones, not the hairlike moss that decorates tree trunks. As you collect, keep moss patches moist by placing them in plastic bags.

Position the moss patches on top of the moistened soil surface of your bonsai, fitting them together like pieces of a puzzle. Scrape off any excess soil you collected, leaving just enough to hold the moss together. Lightly press down the moss pieces to ensure contact with the soil in the bonsai container. When the moss is in place, moisten it with a fine spray of water.

Rocky terrain

Different kinds of rocks create different effects. Before you go rock hunting, though, consider whether a rock will add materially to the spirit of your bonsai or merely clutter its simplicity. If you do decide to add a rock, here are a few guidelines to help you select the right one.

Many pine, spruce, and other needle-leafed or coniferous evergreens grow naturally in the company of rocks—often on high, rocky slopes where rain and wind have stripped away much

of the soil. Rocks here seem to be thrusting directly up from the earth, with sharp angles, jagged edges, and deep clefts. For bonsai plants that are native to such settings, use rocks that reflect the natural landscape. Don't add smooth stones or simply rest rocks on the soil surface.

Broad-leafed trees, both deciduous and evergreen, hail from lower elevations where climate often is more temperate than in the realm of much of the needle-leafed clan. Any rocks found here usually have softer and rounder contours that reflect the more gentle sculpting of rainfall or perhaps glaciation.

Willows, alders, and other trees found in lowlands and along watercourses are naturally associated with smooth stones that have been contoured by running water.

Artistic judgment and discretion determine whether you should use one or more rocks. If you do use more than one, be sure to select rocks of the same type. Try to arrange them so that the grains are running in the same direction. When you use more than one rock, they should appear to be part of a single geological formation rather than several unrelated objects.

Smoothly rounded rocks suggest a terrain where running water or glacial action has formed the contours.

RAFT & ROCK PLANTING

These three bonsai styles entail more than simply placing a selected plant in a container. The initial effort may seem painstaking, but the results justify the extra work.

Raft-style bonsai

A Raft bonsai differs from a Group Planting (see page 30) in one important respect: all plants in this grove stem from the same root system. This style imitates the forest tree that continues to flourish after it has toppled. To achieve this effect in bonsai, you plant a tree on its side and allow select branches to become the grove.

To create a Raft bonsai, select a plant that has a well-developed trunk and several vigorous branches growing from one side of the trunk. Cut off all other branches, leaving just small stubs. Then wire the remaining branches so they point generally in the same direction; these will be the "trees" of the finished raft. Trim and thin out roots (see page 50).

In a shallow oval or rectangular pot, position the plant with the roots at one end of the pot, branches pointing up, and the trunk flush with the soil. Then flatten the thinned-out root ball into the soil, cutting out roots that point upward. Wire the root mass into place, then cover it with soil. Bring the soil level up to the trunk, but don't cover it.

In time, each branch will develop into a separate trunk, and the ensemble will resemble a grove of trees. Each of these "trees" may even develop its own set of roots in time.

Rock-planted bonsai

Two of the styles described on pages 30–31 depend on rock as an important element in the composition. In the Clinging to Rock design, the rock serves as a container; in the Root over Rock style, the roots envelop the rock on their descent into the soil in the bonsai container.

Clinging to Rock. Depending on its shape, a craggy rock may offer anchorage for one or more plants. Determine how many plants your selected rock will accommodate. Then assemble

For Root over Rock planting, cover roots and rock surface with peat muck, then position plant on rock.

After plant is in place on rock, secure it by wrapping roots to the rock with raffia. Mist frequently to keep moist.

these materials: your plant or plants, "peat muck," string or wire, and sphagnum moss.

Functioning as both adhesive and soil, peat muck is indispensable. You make it by combining equal parts peat moss and clay soil, adding just enough water to work it into a pasty condition that feels like slightly gritty modeling clay.

When you have prepared the peat muck, remove all soil from around the roots of your plant. Untangle the roots and trim them, as needed, to fit the rock. Spread peat muck over the rock; then position the plant on the rock, spreading the roots over the rock's contours. Tuck the roots into any pockets or crevices in the rock, then cover them with peat muck.

After the roots are covered, place a moisture-retentive material over the peat muck to keep it damp. Sphagnum moss is readily available and easy to work with. Wet it thoroughly in a bowl or pail of water, squeeze out any excess water, and place a thin layer over the peat muck. Tie it in place with string or thin-gauge copper wire wound around the rock. Mist daily to keep the moss and peat muck moist.

Finished planting has lower one-fourth of rock beneath soil in container; lower roots extend beneath the soil.

After one full growing season or one year, the plant should have adapted to its rocky perch. You can then remove the string or wire and the sphagnum moss covering. Moisten the peat muck regularly, using mist from a spray bottle or the fine-spray head of a watering can. In time, much of the peat muck will wash away, exposing the rock and much of the root system.

Root over Rock. In this style, shown on the front cover, a craggy rock protrudes from a soil-filled bonsai container. The plant's roots form a tracery over the rock as they grow down into the soil. It's easiest to work with plants that have had their roots trained in narrow pots (see "Exposed Root" on page 37).

Wash all soil from the roots, place the plant on the rock covered with peat muck, then drape the roots over the rock. You want the roots to cling closely to the rock's contours, so don't trim them except to enhance the fit. After working the roots into cracks and crevices, cover them with peat muck. If they won't cling to the rock, wrap them with string or raffia, and apply more peat muck.

Once you've secured the plant, place the rock in the bonsai container. Partially fill the container with potting soil so that about one-fourth of the rock will be below the surface of the soil. Spread out the roots that will be covered, then fill the container with soil.

You can cover the peat muck with sphagnum moss to conserve moisture, or surround the planted rock with a bottomless container— such as a cut-down milk carton (see page 37)— filled with enough potting soil to cover the roots. After a year or so, when the plant is established, remove the moss or the bottomless container and the soil it held.

Continued watering of the peat muck will gradually wash it away, leaving an exposed network of roots that will draw its sustenance from the soil of the bonsai container.

Care & Training

PLANT NEEDS & SHAPING TECHNIQUES

A *persistent misconception exists that bonsai plants are touchy, difficult to maintain, and quick to perish with just the slightest inattention to their special needs. In reality, this is far from true. If you remember that the word "bonsai" roughly translates as "plant in a pot," you'll understand that these plants have basically the same needs as other container plantings. In the next 18 pages you'll first learn how to care for a bonsai and then move on to the very heart of the bonsai art: training the plant.*

Pinus thunbergiana (Japanese black pine) demonstrates the ultimate in training: wired limbs, weights, wedge and belt for adjusting branch spread.

BASIC CARE FOR BONSAI

The elements of bonsai care are familiar to anyone who grows container plants—proper location, water, fertilizer, and pest control. But because the growth of bonsai plants is so carefully regulated, each of these elements takes on a special slant.

Collector's "bonsai garden" includes sunny and shaded display areas plus a table-height workbench.

LOCATION

Though you may want to display a specimen indoors for special occasions, the most important point to grasp is that a bonsai is not a house plant. Indoor temperature and humidity levels and inadequate light can seriously erode the health of a bonsai plant in a very short time. Keep these plants outside where they can thrive on fresh air, sunlight, and normal atmospheric moisture.

When you look for just the right outdoor site for your bonsai, the watchword is "moderate." Avoid exposing a plant to any extremes of weather—excessive heat, high winds, and torrential rain.

Place bonsai where they will receive as much sunlight as possible without overheating or burning. This will vary according to the kind of climate you have where you live.

Where overcast and cool days are common, a spot that receives full sunlight may be a suitable bonsai home. In sunnier, warmer regions, give plants the best possible light while sheltering them from the intense sun of summer afternoons. In these hot and sunny areas, a high-branching tree might provide adequate shade for a bonsai. But if you lack a natural sun block, you can build a simple structure that will filter sunlight through latticework, bamboo screens, or shade cloth. Never place plants where they might be overheated by sun reflecting off a nearby wall.

Choose a growing site that permits free air circulation yet shelters your bonsai from strong winds. A breeze can be good, a wind damaging or even fatal to bonsai. Also make sure that plants will be protected from direct, pelting rain in the spot you choose for them—or have an alternate spot to which you can move the bonsai during downpours.

Animals, both domestic and wild, can damage unprotected plants. It's a good idea to keep bonsai plants raised on benches or tables where they won't be routinely exposed to house pets. If squirrels, raccoons, or deer are common visitors to your garden, you may need to position your bonsai someplace where these animals have no access.

WATERING

Because a bonsai grows in a small container, there is a limited amount of soil to hold water. Regular watering is thus a priority. How frequently do you need to water? The answer depends on the size and type of plant, the soil volume, and the weather.

When to water

With larger plants in proportionately larger containers, you may be able to stretch the intervals between watering, unless the soil is so infiltrated by roots that it dries out quickly. Maples and other deciduous plants with thin leaves usually need more frequent watering than needle-leafed conifers such as pines and junipers.

Watering requirements are affected by changes in the weather. During hot periods, you may need to water at least twice a day, in the morning and again in late afternoon or early evening. Plants transpire water rapidly through their leaves during hot weather, and evaporation of moisture from the soil is also high. If the weather is cool or cloudy, however, you may only need to water every other day or so.

The amount of daylight influences watering needs, whatever the weather. In equally hot weather, soil will remain moist longer in late summer and early autumn than it does during the long days of summer.

Check your bonsai daily during the growing season. You don't want soil so dry that the plant wilts, but you also don't want soil so moist that the roots die from lack of air. Feel the soil with your fingertips. If it's dry, water right away; if it's just slightly moist, water before it dries out completely. When the soil feels cool and damp, you can safely wait a while before watering, weather permitting.

How to water

You can't go wrong by using a traditional watering can with a fine-spray head at the end of a long spout. You can water both the foliage and the soil by simply waving the can up and down

Electronic controller automatically runs a watering system according to frequency and duration of your choosing.

over the plant. This keeps foliage free of dust, helps control certain pests, and allows the plant to absorb some moisture through its leaves. To ensure that the entire soil mass becomes well moistened, keep applying water to the surface until it begins to run out of the container's drainage hole.

You also can water a bonsai by simply plunging the pot into a container of water so that the water comes almost up to the pot's rim. Let it stand for about 15 minutes, or until water has been drawn up into the soil all the way to the top. Routine watering by this method can cause potentially harmful salts to build up in the soil. To flush out impurities, water well from the soil surface at least every week or two. And don't forget to sprinkle foliage frequently.

Whichever watering method you use, if your tap water has high levels of chlorine or other chemical additives you might want to use well water, rain water, or distilled water instead.

Watering a large collection. If you become captivated by bonsai, your collection is bound to grow—in time perhaps becoming too large to water easily by hand. To simplify the watering process for a large collection of bonsai plants, you can set up a simple drip irrigation system with one or more emitters going to each plant (one emitter per pot for small containers, two or more apiece for larger ones). Or encircle each plant with plastic "laser" tubing which emits water through predrilled holes spaced evenly along its length.

You can carry efficiency one step further by setting up an automatically-controlled watering system. An automated setup is no substitute for checking your bonsai plants daily, but it will handle basic watering needs—especially useful for the times you're not there to water. Hardware stores and garden centers stock electronic controllers (popularly called "timers") that will automatically turn a watering system on and off. Simply connect your drip irrigation system to the controller and program it for the watering schedule of your choice. It's an easy matter to step up or cut back on watering frequency as the weather or season changes.

You also can use automated drip irrigation to mist foliage and reduce air temperature. Because the duration and timing of misting will differ from that of watering, you'll need to establish a separate system operated by a separate controller circuit.

Fertilizer pellets specially made for bonsai incorporate soluble nutrients that leach into soil with each watering.

FERTILIZING

It's easy to assume that carefully dwarfed bonsai need no nutrients that might make them grow. But even though you may not want to encourage bonsai to increase much in size, like all plants they must have nourishment to stay healthy and resist disease. Because their roots are concentrated in small amounts of soil and nutrients are leached from that soil by frequent watering, you need to fertilize bonsai regularly.

Some dedicated bonsai enthusiasts make their own fertilizers from various combinations of organic ingredients such as cottonseed meal, blood meal, and bone meal. Bonsai specialty suppliers may even stock fertilizer pellets especially made for bonsai. You place the pellets on the soil surface; watering carries their nutrients into the soil.

The novice bonsai grower, however, will find it easy to apply a liquid fertilizer—either an organic fertilizer such as fish emulsion or one of the many commercially available inorganic fertilizers.

Be cautious when using liquid fertilizer. It's always better to overdilute than underdilute. The safest approach is to use twice the amount of water recommended on the product label,

Simple drip irrigation setup has ½-inch polyvinyl tubing feeder line with microtubing and emitters for each bonsai.

creating a half-strength solution. This avoids any possibility of damaging roots.

A plant needs the most fertilizer during its growing season. Young and maturing specimens should be fertilized with a liquid product high in nitrogen every other week from early spring to midsummer. Older, more mature plants will thrive on the same regime though they can get by with monthly applications. From midsummer to midautumn, use fertilizer high in phosphorus and potassium with little or no nitrogen. Labels state the percentages of these elements in numbers such as 10–5–5, 15–0–0, and 0–10–10. Nitrogen is indicated by the first number, phosphorus (as phosphoric acid) by the second, and potassium (as potash) by the third.

Before you fertilize, be sure the soil is moist from a recent watering. Apply liquid fertilizer during the cool hours of early morning, or wait until later in the afternoon or early evening. Using a watering can with a fine-spray head, apply the solution to the soil until the excess liquid flows out from the pot's drainage hole.

PEST CONTROL

Bonsai plants are subject to the same pests and diseases as their full-sized garden counterparts. But because the plants are small and portable, controlling these problems is much easier.

Considering the broad range of plants used in bonsai, it's difficult to generalize about pests and diseases. A comprehensive garden book will help you to identify a problem and will recommend appropriate control measures. Or you can take the plant to a reliable nursery or garden center for diagnosis. The most common problem pests are aphids (particularly in spring), spider mites (in summer), scale, and mealybugs. Slugs and snails can also damage some plants.

To control pests, try the easiest method first. Simply remove larger pests by hand. Smaller ones, such as aphids and mites, can be hosed off with a spray of water. Repeat the process several times at 2- to 3-day intervals.

If you choose a pest-control spray other than water, try one that is the least dangerous to organisms other than the target pest. A solu-

Simple, hand-held spray bottle is easy applicator of water-soluble pesticides to individual bonsai specimens.

tion of insecticidal soap or liquid dishwashing detergent (2 tablespoons in 1 gallon of water) will kill soft-bodied insects and the larva stage of scale insects. The solution kills by contact, so a thorough application is necessary. Rinse off the plant with water about an hour after you use a soap spray. Light horticultural oils, called "summer oils," operate in the same manner and are equally effective.

If you decide to use a stronger commercial pesticide, you have a choice of botanical insecticides (made from plants) or synthetics. Read labels to determine what the product kills beyond your intended target, then use the one that causes the least amount of collateral damage. Also check the product's residual life.

Disease control options are continually changing. New products come on the market as others are withdrawn. Consult a reputable nursery or your county agricultural agent to learn about the latest and most effective control for your particular problem.

No matter what type of spray you use for pests and diseases, make sure the bonsai is well watered before you apply it. Move the plant to a shaded area, and spray in the cool hours of early morning or late in the day.

TOOLS FOR TRAINING & MAINTAINING BONSAI

Dedicated bonsai growers use an array of pruning and grooming tools. Some are familiar items not originally intended for bonsai use, but others have been designed especially for training and taking care of bonsai plants.

Most of the specialized tools are for pruning. Because bonsai specimens are smaller than most ordinary garden plants and subject to close scrutiny, you need tools that make clean, inconspicuous cuts in tight spaces. Most ordinary garden instruments are simply too large and clumsy for bonsai work.

Special bonsai tools

Pruning shears head the list of specialty bonsai items. The *long-bladed pruner* shown in the photo at right (A) will remove twigs and succulent new growth, and it is good for cutting leaves. It's particularly well designed to reach into cramped spaces. The *shorter-bladed shears* in the photo (B) also can trim twigs, new growth, and leaves, as well as cut exposed roots. The shorter, stouter blades give this tool more cutting power.

Pincers-type instruments (C–G) leave a slightly concave depression when they cut. Use these tools to minimize scarring when cutting branches. They come in various sizes, depending on the bite you need to take.

Ordinary tools

Several standard household items are useful in bonsai maintenance. *Hook-and-blade shears* (H, I) are good for routine pruning as long as you keep them sharp. These pointed-blade styles are handier in close quarters than the familiar curved-blade type.

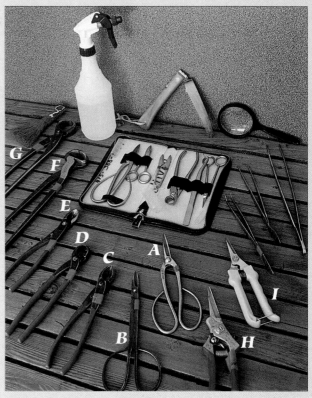

Array of bonsai tools includes basic kit (center), tweezers, magnifying glass to detect insects, spray bottle, whisk broom, and various pruning devices.

A *pruning saw* removes branches too thick for shears. It's particularly useful in shaping large plants collected from the wild. *Tweezers* will pull out the occasional weed seedling, pick off debris and large pests, and even remove unwanted buds and new shoots.

A *whisk broom* with soft bristles serves to brush away dust and small particles from soil or moss. A *magnifying glass* lets you check for microscopic pests such as spider mites. A *spray bottle* can be used to apply insecticide spray and to moisten foliage.

TRAINING TECHNIQUES

Historically, bonsai specimens were shaped by their environment. Collectors would dig naturally sculpted plants from the wild and pot them—at which point they became bonsai. But today, most bonsai plants are developed by careful training that mimics nature's shaping.

Bonsai are trained both by regulating growth and by directing the shape in which a plant grows. It is in this phase of bonsai culture that a knowledge of plants must come together with artistic sensibility in order to create a successful specimen.

TRAINING BONSAI BY REGULATING GROWTH

Gardeners are quite familiar with manipulating plant growth by pinching and pruning. The chief difference in these two methods is that you pinch soft growth but prune hard, woody stems. With leaf cutting, another type of plant control, you remove leaves to promote more growth.

In general gardening, pinching is usually done to keep potentially leggy plants compact and bushy. Pinching out the soft growing tip of a stem redirects the growth into buds just below the pinch, resulting in two or more new stems branching off the original stem.

Pruning, on the other hand, removes mature branches that are part of a plant's structure. Pruning may be done to stimulate branching growth from beneath a cut, to simplify a plant's structure, or to change its shape.

You pinch and prune bonsai for just the same reasons. The main difference is in the magnitude of the effect. Each pinch of a bonsai can make a significant difference in the plant's development; each pruned branch irrevocably alters the form of the plant.

Thumb and forefinger are primary pruning tools, always available to pinch out tips of soft new growth.

Pinching

If you start with a small, young plant, you'll probably be able to do a great deal of the shaping you want by pinching. Pinching will control the direction of new growth. As a general rule, you want to pinch out much of the new growth that would grow toward the plant's interior, cluttering the plant's structure. Pinch out tips of growing stems to create branching where you want it. Unwanted growth that starts to sprout from a branch or trunk can simply be rubbed off with your fingers.

Generally speaking, you can pinch out new growth as needed anytime during the growing season. Depending on the plant and the time of year, new growth may appear beneath the pinch within several weeks or may wait until the next growing season.

Thumb and forefinger are the gardener's traditional pinching tools. But you may need more delicate instruments for bonsai. Tweezers can enable you to pinch out the smallest, softest growth. Cuticle scissors or small bonsai trimmers (see page 62) will make it easier to cut cleanly in tight spaces.

Pruning

To alter the shape of a bonsai or to simplify its structure, you'll need to do a certain amount of pruning.

Minor pruning consists of cutting out any unnecessary small branches so that a plant's structure is more clearly visible. This type of

Made for bonsai work, these concave cutters will remove branches and leave a concave wound to minimize scarring.

pruning can be an annual event or an ongoing activity if you have plants that produce dense, leafy growth throughout the year.

Major pruning, on the other hand, involves removing entire branches to effect a more dramatic change. In general, this is a one-time operation performed only when converting nursery stock or plants collected from the wild into bonsai specimens. This initial pruning establishes a plant's basic shape by removing nonessential and unattractive branches. Further development is controlled by minor pruning, pinching, and wiring (see page 65).

With major pruning there's no turning back. Once a branch is removed, it's gone for good. So study the plant carefully, analyzing its potential shape, before you make any major alterations. Most major pruning is best done toward the end of a plant's dormant period, usually in late winter or early spring.

To prevent or minimize bark scarring from major pruning, use sharp pruning shears to make clean cuts. Special branch cutters that leave a slightly concave indentation (see photo at left) are best for removing branches. The indentation becomes virtually flat when bark eventually grows to cover the cut.

As a general rule, don't make a cut that leaves a branch stub attached. Usually the stub is unattractive, and it may die back within the branch or trunk onto which it is attached, leavin the area vulnerable to decay. An exception to the rule occurs with certain conifers (such as junipers) which may look authentically rugged with the remains of old branches attached.

Leaf cutting

The simple technique of leaf cutting can be judiciously used on healthy broad-leafed evergreen and deciduous plants. It may accelerate growth and reduce the size of a plant's leaves.

Leaf cutting is actually defoliation of a plant. By removing all of a plant's leaves, you create a false autumn. Because you do this during the growing season, the plant soon begins putting out new growth. What you've done is to squeeze two growing seasons into one, more quickly adding size to young plants.

Leaf cutting will cause plant to produce another burst of new growth; remove entire leaf, leaving just leaf stalk.

Leaf cutting won't significantly affect leaf size on young plants. If practiced on older, established bonsai specimens, however, it may substantially reduce the size of the foliage.

When you do leaf cutting, make sure that the entire leaf is removed, leaving only the leaf stalk (petiole), as shown in the photo above. If any portion of the leaf itself remains, the plant will concentrate its energy on maintaining the leaf fragment instead of putting out new growth.

The time for leaf cutting is from late spring through midsummer. Cut early in this period in regions with long growing seasons, later where seasons are short. The first leaves should be somewhat mature so the second set won't grow with greater vigor. If you remove leaves too early in spring (before the end of May), the second-growth leaves may be larger than the first crop. If you wait to defoliate deciduous plants until late summer, the plant may enter dormancy early without putting out further leaves.

New leaves should start to appear about 4 weeks after you remove the first set. Until new growth buds swell, keep the bonsai in a well-lighted, shaded location. Without leaves transpiring moisture, the bonsai will need less frequent watering than it did in full leaf.

TRAINING BONSAI BY WIRING

Beyond the standard gardening methods of pinching and pruning to influence plant form, bonsai artists utilize a technique unique to bonsai—wiring. While pinching and pruning remove superfluous growth to affect a plant's shape, wiring redirects existing growth, literally forcing branches to grow in the directions and positions you desire. Wiring can achieve such remarkable transformations as turning a naturally upright plant into a Cascade, or making a sinuous trunk out of a straight one.

Wiring must be done with care, as wire is more flexible than the branches it will guide. Wire will always bend; branches may break. Before you tackle a bonsai plant, it's wise to practice the wiring technique on fairly limber branches cut from garden trees or shrubs.

When to wire

The best time for wiring varies according to the kind of plant. In general, deciduous plants should be wired during the growing season after new leaves have reached their full size. Branches are more limber at this time. All evergreens can be wired in winter so that wires are in place before next spring's growth.

Don't attempt to wire soft, new growth; wait until it has firmed up the following year. And avoid wiring plants while they're putting on new growth which could be damaged in the process.

What wire to use

Though copper is the traditional wire used in bonsai, aluminum wire with a dull finish is growing in popularity. Aluminum wire comes ready to use, is always flexible, holds bends well, and isn't affected by the elements. Copper needs to be treated before you use it, and it's much less flexible once it has been used.

However, if you prefer the warm color of copper wire and the patina of oxidation it acquires as it ages, you can make it more flexible

Wire thickness is expressed in gauge numbers—the smaller the number, the thicker the wire. Number 8 wire is heavy and should be used only for a trunk. Number 16 wire is light and should be used for very thin branches or for tying (see page 71). Because aluminum wire is more flexible than copper wire, you'll have to use thicker gauges to hold bends if you are using aluminum.

For each branch to be wired, you'll need a piece of wire about 1½ times as long as the section you will be wiring.

Advance work

Before you wire a plant, withhold water for a day or two to make the branches a bit more flexible. Just before you're ready to start wiring, test the limberness of the branches by gently bending each one in the direction of the curve you plan to establish with the wire.

Coils of copper wire in a variety of gauges—annealed, oxidized, and ready for use.

by the process of annealing. Simply make a fire of tightly wrapped newspapers and place the coil of wire in the fire. After the flames have turned blue, remove the wire and let it cool. Don't unwind or bend the treated wire until you are ready to use it.

You can buy wire at nurseries, garden centers, and hardware stores. The size you need depends on the thickness of the branch or trunk you plan to wire. Thicker branches will require the heaviest wire; slender, pliable branches can be held in position with thinner wire. Use the lightest-weight wire you can to do the job.

To offset injury to thin-barked plants, wrap limbs to be wired in raffia before applying wire.

Wrap wire in a continuous diagonal spiral, from base to tip, keeping a uniform space between coils.

If a branch bends as far as you want, you should be able to wire it into that position. If you encounter resistance, however, further bending will likely cause the branch to break. In that case, plan on making the bend in stages over several years of training.

To avoid bruising or scarring branches of thin-barked plants such as azaleas and maples, cover the wires with paper tape before you wrap them around the branches. Where wire will apply much pressure to a bend, wrap the branch with raffia to pad it.

How to wire

Before a wire can be bent firmly into place, it must be securely anchored. Always begin below the lowest point to be trained and work upward. To shape the trunk or lower branches, anchor the wire in the soil, pushing it down to the bottom of the container at the back of the plant. To train higher branches, secure the wire by wrapping it around the trunk below the lowest branch to be shaped. Start and stop all wiring on the back side of the trunk or branches.

Wrap the wire, either clockwise or counterclockwise, in an upward spiral at about a 45° angle, maintaining a uniform distance between coils. The wire will tighten as you bend the branches, so keep it snug but not too tight. If it's too loose, the wire won't hold a bend; if it's

too tight, it will damage the bark. That's why it's a good idea to practice on a cut branch.

When you move from wiring the trunk to wiring branches on a plant, you can use the same wire if the branches are nearly as sturdy as the trunk. But if the branches are distinctly less robust, finish off the trunk with the heavier wire, then switch to a lighter gauge for the smaller branches.

Use one hand to guide the wire around the branch and the other hand to hold the coils you have already made tightly in place. As you progress outward on a branch, begin bending it the way you want it to go. Once the branch is completely wired, you can make the final bend. Hold the branch firmly and place both thumbs together on the inside of the bend. Gradually bend the branch into position. Be sure that there is wire coiling on the outside of the bend to hold it in place.

Continued on page 70

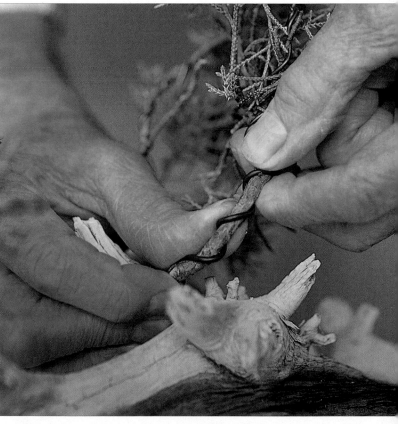

Use thumb pressure to bend a wired branch, being sure that the wire coils over the outside of the bend.

CHRYSANTHEMUM BONSAI

Most bonsai are fashioned from trees and shrubs with long-lived, woody structures. Still, it's no surprise that Asian bonsai artisans also turned their skills toward training their best-loved flowering perennial, the chrysanthemum.

To create bonsai from chrysanthemums, you need plants with small flowers and foliage. The best candidates are short, compact, and flexible plants that branch profusely, have short internodes (lengths of stem between leaves) and flower stems, and produce strong roots. Some chrysanthemum growers offer named cultivars that are proven bonsai successes.

Early autumn is the best time to take cuttings. They will root quickly and give you strong, husky plants by flowering time the next autumn. Root 4-inch softwood cuttings as described on page 42. After they're well rooted (4 to 6 weeks), you can cut them back a bit to encourage growth at the base. The shoots for bonsai training come from this growth.

Winter work

In early winter (late autumn in mild regions), transfer rooted cuttings to individual 3- or 4-inch pots. A good potting soil can be made from 5 parts compost or commercial potting mix, 3 parts good garden soil, and 1 part sand. When potting, spread the roots out evenly in an attractive radial pattern that can be partially exposed in the finished bonsai.

In cold-winter climates, place rooted cuttings in a cool greenhouse or other sheltered location to keep the soil from freezing. Giving young plants added light during the coldest months encourages their development. Using a 60-watt bulb set 3 feet above the plant, illuminate plants for 4 hours, starting at dusk. Continue nightly from January to mid-April.

In regions where the growing season is long, you can take cuttings in mid- to late win-

Well-groomed Double Trunk specimen features an entire trunk of picturesque "jin" (see page 74).

ter and still get good results by autumn. Simply pot the rooted cuttings, then train the strongest stem or stems growing from the base.

Spring training

Begin training as soon as new growth gets underway—as early as late winter in mild-winter regions. Keep the plant growing rapidly but not rankly, developing a thick, sturdy structure. You don't want long shoots and great plant enlargement. Be sure to rotate pots regularly so growth will develop evenly on all sides.

Repotting. About every 6 weeks, you'll need to repot each plant. Roots will have filled the container by then, showing clearly at the drainage hole. At each repotting, shift the plant to a slightly larger clay pot. In regions with long growing seasons and warm springs, you may need to cut away up to one-third of the bottom of the root ball each time you repot to keep the plant from becoming too large.

Pinching & pruning. From late winter or early spring (depending on climate) to midsummer, pay close attention to pinching and pruning. Pinching produces branching, limits plant size, and encourages thickening of trunks and branches; pruning removes superfluous growth.

Begin pinching in late winter or early spring and continue about every 3½ weeks. Each time, remove ½ inch of tip growth on each stem. (If you want a stem to lengthen, train the uppermost new growth to continue the extension.) The first pinch promotes low growth that will be part of the permanent plant structure. Additional pinching develops the structure and hastens stem thickening.

As the plant develops, prune out all growth that will not be part of the final bonsai. To help thicken the trunk, let several extra branches develop low on the trunk. Prune these out by late spring. Remove large leaves that grow in the interior of the plant; they can shade developing branches, making them grow long and spindly.

Structural training. When branches reach 3 to 4 inches long, you can start training for style. Bend stems when they're young and flexible; as they mature, they become stiff and brittle.

To direct growth, you can wire plants as they grow, following the techniques outlined on pages 65–67. Or form the shape you want from 12-gauge wire and tie the stems to it as they grow. If you use traditional wiring methods, rewire with 12- to 18-gauge wire about every month to avoid wire scars as stems thicken. You also can use weights (see page 72) to direct growth.

Summer to autumn

If plants grow too rapidly and get leggy, move them to sunnier locations, cut back on fertilizer, and apply water only to the soil. In early to mid-August (the earlier time in cold-winter regions), pinch all growth tips one more time. The stems that then develop will produce autumn flowers; any unnecessary growth can be removed later. Also, prune out stems that won't be part of the final composition.

To get uniform flowering, you'll need to perform a final three-stage pinch. First, pinch back all secondary branches in the lower one-third of the plant to two leaves. Three days later, do the same to secondary branches in the center of the plant. After four more days, pinch back all remaining upper branches. If you start this during the first week of September, you'll get uniform flowering around the first of November.

As flower buds appear on stems following the three-stage pinch, remove all but one on each stem—usually the center bud. Make sure that all remaining buds are the same size. If you didn't perform the three-part pinch, thin bud clusters to one bud apiece at this time, choosing buds of the same size.

Leave the plant in its pot while flower buds are forming. Then after you've thinned the buds, you can finally pot the plant in its bonsai container.

Another year?

With proper treatment, your chrysanthemum bonsai may live for one or more additional years. Cut off blossoms as they begin to fade, even before they wilt. In late autumn, cut back all branches that aren't part of the defining structure, leaving only two or three leaves per branch. During the winter, keep the plant in a sunny spot where the temperature remains above freezing, and water sparingly.

When new growth buds emerge, you may be able to build upon the previous year's structure. At worst, you'll get a number of new shoots that can be treated as cuttings or detached with a bit of root and grown as new plants.

Dealing with breaks

Even if you are careful, you may bend a branch to its breaking point while wiring. If the break is simply a fracture with the broken part still partially attached, you have a chance of saving the branch. Very gently ease the broken part into place, carefully fitting both ends of the break together. Wrap the break with garden tape or raffia and tie it securely but not too tightly.

Wire scars result when wire remains in place more than one growing season while branch diameter increases.

Within several months, the fractured branch tissue may knit together.

If the break is complete or the ends fail to unite, you have several choices. You can cut the broken branch back to where side branches grow out from it or you can cut it back to its point of origin. You might even consider making the branch into *jin* (see page 74).

Care after wiring

To help your bonsai recover from the trauma of wiring, keep it out of direct sunlight for several days. It's also a good idea to keep it sheltered from wind for several weeks. Water the plant routinely, giving the foliage a daily sprinkling.

Removing the wire

To give wired branches a good chance to grow into their new positions, leave wires in place for a full growing season. Then, in early autumn, remove them to avoid any constriction during the next growth phase. If wires are left in place too long, the bark will show unsightly spiral scars for years. With stiff copper wire, it is best to cut it carefully from branches to avoid inflicting damage by uncoiling. Aluminum wire can be uncoiled, starting at the outermost end and carefully uncoiling toward the anchor end.

If wired branches still need more coaxing to achieve the desired positions, they can be rewired at the appropriate time for another year of training. When you rewire a branch, vary the wire position from that of the previous year. You may be able to reuse aluminum wire. Straighten bends and twists by hand, then flatten any remaining kinks by tapping the wire with a mallet.

ADDITIONAL TRAINING TECHNIQUES

Before wiring became standard practice, bonsai practitioners manipulated the shapes of their plants in other ways. These methods lack the

When wiring a branch to a trunk or pot, prevent scarring by padding the wire where it pulls against the branch.

To enhance a branch's simple downward inclination, suspend a weight from the branch.

relative unobtrusiveness of wire, but they are still effective training techniques.

Bending branches

If you need to make a simple downward bend in a branch, there are three reasonably easy ways to do it.

Tying to the trunk. Branches too stiff to bend by wiring can often be bent by tying. You simply attach wire to the branch, bend the branch down, and tie the wire to the trunk. You can use a thinner gauge of wire for tying than for wiring a bend.

Encircle the branch with a loose wire loop, protecting the wood by slipping padding (such as cloth, paper, or rubber) between the branch and the wire. Also place padding between the

wire and the trunk where the wire exerts pressure against the trunk.

Make the bend gradually in order to avoid breaking the limb. Start by pulling the limb about one-third of the way toward its desired position. After 2 to 3 months, bend the branch a bit more, and then give it more time to adjust to that position. Repeat this process until you eventually achieve the bend you desire.

Tying to the container. You can also wire branches to the plant's container to pull them downward.

Loop a strand of wire under the pot and up over the soil, then tie the ends together snugly. Now run a separate loop of padded wire from each branch that you wish to bend down to the wire that goes across the pot. Pull down on the wire until the branch is in the position you want, then secure the branch wire to the pot wire. As with the previous method, it's best to do this in gradual stages so that the branch doesn't break.

Weighting a branch. A third way to bend a branch down is to attach a weight to it. Fishing weights suspended from the branch by a string are traditional, but any object heavy enough to exert the desired pressure will work. Choose the weight with care—if it's too heavy, it may break the branch. Don't use this method if your bonsai plant is in a breezy location; in a wind, weighted branches can pump up and down to the breaking point.

Spreading & snugging

If your bonsai has a pair of branches or trunks that are either too close together or too far apart and you can't separate them by wiring, these two training methods offer a simple solution to the problem.

Spreading. A simple wedge can permanently spread apart two branches that are growing too

To widen the distance between two branches, insert a wooden wedge between them.

If two branches should grow closer together for better appearance, simply use a belt to narrow the distance.

close. This works particularly well to separate parallel trunks and forked branches.

Take a small piece of wood, cut it into a triangular or trapezoidal shape, and gently wedge it between the limbs until they are separated as far as you want. Be very careful when separating forked branches; too much pressure can cause a split down the fork.

Remove the wedge after 4 months. If the branches return to their original positions, put the wedge back in place. Eventually the branches will lose their tendency to spring back when you take away the wedge.

Snugging. To bring two branches closer, especially parallel ones, loop a soft cord or a small belt around them and pull them into the desired position. Or form a piece of sturdy wire into an "S" shape, hooking each branch into one of the curves of the "S." In time, the branches will stay in place on their own.

REPOTTING

While it's possible to keep a bonsai in the same container for many years, you'll need to prune the roots and repot the plant periodically to keep it healthy.

Over time, soil quality deteriorates: organic matter breaks down, leaving compacted soil that drains poorly. Also, the plant becomes rootbound—at which point growth will slow or stop. Even stepped-up watering and feeding won't prevent decline. By simply repotting, you can replace soil and reduce root mass to ensure the growth of new feeder roots.

Late winter, before growth begins, is a good time to check for rootbound plants. Withhold water for a day or so, letting the soil dry a bit so that the root ball will remain intact when you remove it from its pot. Insert a spatula between the root ball and the pot edge to loosen the root mass. If that doesn't do the job, use a chopstick to loosen soil around the edge. Then gently lift out the plant.

Look at the soil mass. If you see nothing but packed roots, you know it's time to revital-

Tease apart root mass with chopsticks, untangle roots and shorten thick ones, then cut back all as for initial potting.

ize the plant and the soil. But if you see a fair amount of soil between the roots (or soil with few roots), return the plant to the pot, water it, and leave it for another year or two.

If your bonsai grows on a rock or among several rocks, you won't be able to remove it easily. Instead, look at the root density around the edge of the pot and in the drainage holes.

Repotting basics

If your root inspection shows it's time for repotting, take shears or a knife and cut away one-third of the root ball, both soil and roots. Then take a chopstick or other slender, blunt instrument and tease about half of the remaining soil from the roots. Cut back all large roots and any that grow straight down.

Your goal is to flatten the root mass on the bottom and cut it back so that its final thickness is about one-third to one-half the depth of the container. Cut from the sides, too, so that the root ball spread encompasses about two-thirds of the container's surface area. Finally, replant the specimen in its pot with new soil and begin follow-up care, as described on pages 48–52.

Rootbound bonsai ready for repotting will come out of pot easily, revealing solid mass of roots with little soil.

$\mathcal{A}$RTIFICIAL AGE . . . ◆ ◆ ◆

$\mathbf{I}$n nature, the ravages of time and weather produce picturesque specimen trees that appear to be barely clinging to life. The wind-twisted remnants seem to consist mostly of dead snags where limbs once grew, sprouting only a few fingers of live foliage.

These patriarchs of the wild serve as models for some of the most dramatic bonsai plants—specimens with contorted limbs that suggest mountaintops, sea cliffs, and primeval forces of nature. But you don't need hundreds of years and hurricane-force winds to create such seemingly ancient bonsai, just a few special materials, an artistic eye, and courage.

Aged appearance of Juniperus occidentalis (western juniper) is enhanced by jagged snag of jin.

Bonsai artists have applied artificial aging processes to a variety of trees, but coniferous evergreens are favorite subjects. Pines and junipers respond well to these treatments and look particularly convincing.

Before you try either of the following techniques on your bonsai, practice making cuts and peeling bark from cut branches of garden trees or shrubs. The best time of year to perform this reverse cosmetic surgery is early to midspring when plants grow actively and the weather is still fairly cool. Keep postoperative plants in a well-lighted but sheltered location for a month.

Jin

When the bark is stripped off the end of a branch to create a dead branch or snag, Japanese bonsai artists refer to it as *jin*. Artificially creating dead wood in this manner gives a bonsai the look of great age.

To create jin, cut entirely around the branch at the point you want the deadwood to begin. Make the cut deep enough to go through the bark and the cambium layer just beneath, but not so deep as to cut into the woody tissue. Use a sharp penknife or pocket knife. If the entire branch is to be "jinned," cut bark cleanly at the branch's base where it joins a branch or trunk. If you want jin on just the outermost part of a branch, make the cut edge jagged and irregular so the juncture between live and dead wood will appear natural.

When the cut is complete, carefully remove the bark by peeling it back from the tip of the branch to the cut. The wood you expose will die and eventually turn gray.

To create a jagged snag of wood similar to a broken branch stub in the wild, first cut the limb to the desired length, cutting straight across the branch. Then cut the bark as already

JIN & SHARI

Viewed at close range, jin deadwood has weathered and bleached look found in driftwood and on timberline trees.

described and peel it off the cut branch as far back as the trunk. Next, use pruning shears to make two cuts in the form of a cross about 1½ inches deep into the end of the branch. Tear each of the four sections of the cut end back toward the trunk with a concave branch cutter or a pair of needle-nose pliers.

You can leave this jagged stub to weather naturally over time, or you can hasten the discoloration that suggests age by brushing on a lime-sulfur solution (sold at nurseries or garden centers as a dormant spray for fruit trees). Wait 6 to 8 weeks before you use this treatment, and be careful not to get the solution on any live plant tissue.

Shari

If the bark is stripped off part of the trunk of your bonsai, you've created *shari*. This gives the effect of live branches clinging to a half-dead tree or shrub.

Shari is a bit trickier than jin because you must consider all the consequences in advance and plan the deadwood sections so that they flow into the plant's natural form. Will the removal of the trunk's bark jeopardize any branches? Will the cutting be difficult to do?

When you've decided just what part of the bark you want to remove, take a sharp-tipped knife and cut through the bark and cambium layer. Leave a surgically clean cut edge, and be careful not to cut into the woody tissue. Pry up one edge of the bark and strip it from within the cut lines down to the woody tissue.

If you want to artificially weather the shari, wait until the following spring to apply a lime-sulfur solution, as described for jin.

Done with skill and artistry, shari adds to appearance of age while enhancing the plant's natural contours.

Bonsai on Display

AN ART GALLERY FOR YOUR PLANTS

**B**onsai plants have much in common with both works of art and treasured household pets. *Like paintings or sculpture, they are enjoyed for their aesthetic value; and like the family dog, they need tender loving care. Because of their artistic nature, bonsai plants should be positioned where their beauty can be highlighted and appreciated. And to give them the care they need, you'll want to keep them handy so that you can maintain them easily, from routine watering to training. With a bit of thoughtful planning, one location can easily do double duty for display and maintenance.*

Three shelves constructed in bleacher formation hold and display numerous plants while permitting easy access for maintenance.

EFFECTIVE DISPLAY

Any work of art needs a proper showcase so that it can be appreciated to the fullest. The following pages present ideas for long-term outdoor display of your bonsai and for brief highlighting indoors.

OUTDOOR LIFE

If you grow just a few bonsai plants, you will have no problem displaying them. All you need is something that elevates the pots so that you can view them from the front rather than from the top. A patio bench, for example, will accommodate one or several plants.

But when you succumb to the allure of bonsai, you'll soon find your collection outgrowing the original display space. At this point,

One favorite bonsai may deserve a showcase of its own. Semicascade Pinus thunbergiana perches on special table.

you'll want to consider a special setup to showcase the plants.

Benches & shelves

You can put together a simple bonsai bench in a matter of minutes. Select a sturdy wooden plank, such as a 2 by 12, and raise it on concrete blocks, bricks, or flat stones. If you use slats (2 by 2s or 2 by 4s) instead of a single plank, water will drain through the bench.

Another simple display unit is a set of backless shelves. Open shelves permit good air circulation and light penetration.

If you display bonsai on shelves placed against a wall or fence, remember that heat reflection from light-colored walls can seriously damage bonsai plants in summer. Make sure these displays are sheltered from direct sun during the warmest part of the day, usually late morning through afternoon.

Another effective system can be made by mounting three or four shelves like bleachers.

Simple bench displays bonsai specimens, at the same time defining edge of deck and serving as seating.

Set the highest shelf closest to a wall or fence, the next shelf farther out, and so on. This allows water to drain freely without falling on the plants below. Don't make the shelves so deep that you can't reach the plants on top.

Tables

Outdoor tables will certainly hold a collection, but they may not display it to best advantage, since all pots rest on the same level. If you do keep your collection on a table, choose one just wide enough for three plants, then place the larger specimens in the center with smaller plants on the outside rows. Stagger placement so that no plant is directly behind another.

For better display, construct a unit along the lines of a patio table that has built-in benches. Make the center section (table) just wide enough to hold a single or double row of

Single-file lineup against neutral backdrop highlights each specimen while accommodating a collection of plants.

plants; the two lower sections (benches) can be just a bit wider to show off a number of smaller specimens from each side.

Maintenance tips

Don't crowd bonsai plants. You should leave about 8 to 12 inches of space between the outspread branches of adjacent plants so that each plant can develop independently.

Make sure the plants receive at least morning sun, more if climate permits (see page 58). This is particularly important in spring when plants are putting out new growth.

Rotate containers about a quarter of a turn in the same direction every other week to expose all sides to the same conditions. Otherwise, new growth will be strongest on the side facing the light while roots will tend to grow away from the sun. Specimens placed too close to a wall or fence can become one-sided as rear branches dwindle from lack of light.

Rotating small containers is easy; turning larger specimens is more difficult. Use a lazy Susan–type turntable, and you'll be able to turn the largest bonsai with the push of a finger.

Mounted in a sea of gravel, separate pedestal tables display plants in a "bonsai garden."

For special occasions, bonsai can be indoor art. Simple, elegant display table is part of composition.

INDOOR STAY

The temperatures and humidity levels we find comfortable in our homes do not create an agreeable environment for bonsai. Yet the temptation to display these plants indoors is hard to resist. You may simply want to look at them inside on occasion, or share the beauty of choice examples with guests.

How to display

The secrets to successful indoor bonsai display are to limit a stay to 2 days at the most and to be careful where you place plants.

Though plants need plenty of light, don't put them in direct sun. Keep indoor temperature at 70°F/21°C or below, and never place plants near a heating or air-conditioning vent. If possible, open a window to keep the air circulating. Counteract dry indoor air with a humidifier or a pan of water placed near the bonsai.

Thoroughly water a bonsai a few hours before you bring it indoors. After you return the plant to its customary outdoor location, water the soil well and sprinkle the foliage.

Broad-leafed plants, evergreens in particular, usually fare best on indoor visits; needle-leafed evergreens are more sensitive.

Where to display

Low tables with curving legs, pedestals, tree stumps, and highly polished slabs of wood—all make good settings for indoor display of bonsai specimens.

Shops that specialize in Asian decor carry teak and rosewood stands or low tables that work well for plant exhibit. Taller pedestal-type tables show off Cascade bonsai and other Single-Trunk styles to advantage.

A simple indoor display for any but the Cascade style of bonsai can be made by setting a container on a mat of bamboo or woven natural fibers.

For a less formal presentation, you can place individual plants on pedestals of weathered wood or sections of tree trunks. To make the rustic perch more elegant, use stripped and polished stumps or trunks. Cut and polished slices of redwood burl and other wood are other options.

Japanese tokonoma. The Japanese are masters of the minimalist design philosophy. An example of this is the traditional indoor display area called a *tokonoma*—an ideal setting for the brief showcasing of bonsai.

A tokonoma is basically a platform raised a few inches above the regular floor level. A little larger than 3 by 6 feet, it's usually located in an alcove or in the corner of a room. Paintings, decorative scrolls, or calligraphy adorn the wall behind the platform, and a ceramic piece, flower arrangement, bonsai, or other art object is set on the platform itself.

Objects displayed in a tokonoma are carefully chosen and arranged to complement each other without competing for attention. The composition changes periodically to present an ongoing show of art.

WINTER QUARTERS

Container plantings of any kind are more subject to damage from cold than plants growing in the ground. Containers just don't hold enough soil to insulate plant roots.

Some plants, especially broad-leafed evergreens, may die if their roots are exposed to freezing soil temperatures. In fact, frozen soil can be a hazard to any plant that bears leaves throughout winter. Freezing locks up soil moisture, making it impossible for leaves to replace moisture they lose through transpiration.

Where winter temperatures are frost free or relatively mild (above 20°F/-7°C), you can leave a bonsai outside if its normal display area is protected from wind. But where winter lows are in the range of 10°F/-12°C to 20°F/-7°C, surround pots of broad-leafed evergreen bonsai with straw or other lightweight material to insulate the soil and minimize freezing. Plants beneath any kind of overhead, be it house eaves or foliage from a sheltering tree, will remain warmer than plants exposed to open sky.

Winter temperatures that normally fall below 10°F/-12°C can damage or kill many exposed bonsai. Broad-leafed evergreens are the first victims. Needle-leafed evergreens and deciduous plants are more cold-tolerant.

An unheated greenhouse is an ideal winter shelter in cold regions. Plants receive good light, are somewhat protected from the cold, and, with a door ajar or vents open slightly, get plenty of air. You can devise a polyethylene plastic and wood greenhouse by extending a lean-to from under house eaves. Leave all or part of one end open.

Building a cold frame. With just a bit more effort you can build a simple cold frame—essentially a low greenhouse with a translucent hinged top. Placed against a south-facing house wall and recessed into the ground, it will keep plants dormant but not frozen.

Dig a rectangle about 6 to 8 inches deep beside the wall. Using scrap lumber or plywood, build a frame with sides that slope down toward the front; a 6-inch slope is sufficient. Make sure the front is high enough (about 18 inches) to accommodate your shortest bonsai. Then set the frame against the wall and spread 3 to 4 inches of gravel in the bottom.

Traditionally, old window sashes formed the tops of cold frames. But you can cover a wood frame with acrylic plastic, clear fiberglass, or polyethylene plastic sheeting. In snowy areas, first cover the frame with fine-mesh chicken wire or hardware cloth.

Place the bonsai on the gravel base and surround and cover the pots lightly with straw. Close the lid for protection from extreme cold, opening it slightly for ventilation when the temperature is above freezing.

Winter watering. During freezing weather, water your bonsai (if they need it) in the morning. This allows excess water to drain out before the temperature drops. Water-soaked soil expands as it freezes, which can cause containers to crack.

Where winter temperatures dip low enough to endanger plants, a cold frame will overwinter a small collection.

Plants for Bonsai

AN ENCYCLOPEDIA OF SUITABLE TREES & SHRUBS

While experienced practitioners may find almost any plant fair game for bonsai training, novices will benefit from help with initial selections. Some plants are especially easy to work with; some just lend themselves to bonsai—"aging" quickly, bearing foliage in proportion to their dwarfed size, or growing naturally in ways that adapt to certain styles. You'll find recommendations for suitable plants under each bonsai style described on pages 24–37. This chapter profiles those plants along with other popular and proven subjects.

Autumn brings radiant color change to leaves of
Lagerstroemia indica (crape myrtle).

Acer palmatum

ABIES (fir). Evergreen (needle-leafed). In the wild, these mountain dwellers form tall, symmetrical pyramids of layered branches. Needles are short and stiff. Growth habits make them good choices for Formal Upright style and Group Plantings. *Jin* training (see page 74) lends a look of age. Firs grow best in cool, moist climates; they need some winter chill. Prune in spring.

Propagation: seeds.

ACER (maple). Deciduous. Many maples make classic bonsai plants, especially some of the Asian species. New spring growth may be red, pink, or green; autumn foliage turns yellow, orange, red, or maroon. Some selections have bronzy red to maroon leaves rather than green. Most maples grow best where there's a bit of winter chill; leaves may burn where summers are hot and dry. They adapt to a variety of styles and are often used in Group Plantings. Prune in spring, summer.

Japanese maple, *A. palmatum*, is one of two popular choices for bonsai work. In the basic species, leaves are green with 5 to 9 lobes. Many named selections have colored leaves (red to maroon, variegated), finely dissected foliage, or colorful bark. Trident maple, *A. buergeranum*, is the other favorite. Its 3-lobed green leaves turn red, orange, or yellow in autumn.

Other good bonsai maples include *A. campestre* (hedge maple), *A. capillipes*, *A. circinatum* (vine maple), *A. ginnala* (Amur maple), *A. griseum* (paperbark maple), and *A. morrisonense* (Formosan maple).

Propagation: seeds, semihardwood cuttings.

AESCULUS (buckeye, horsechestnut). Deciduous. At first glance, buckeyes may appear to be inappropriate bonsai subjects. Their foliage is almost tropical appearing: each leaf is a fanlike arrangement of 5 to 7 leaflets that grow up to 10 inches long in some species. But with bonsai training, leaf size decreases markedly, and trunks and branches become thick and gnarly. Plants are especially lovely during their leafless period and when the pale green leaves emerge in spring.

For bonsai, look for *A. carnea* (red horsechestnut) and *A. glabra* (Ohio buckeye); *A. californica* (California buckeye) is good in its native territory. Buckeyes are easiest to train in Multiple Trunk styles.

Propagation: seeds.

ALNUS (alder). Deciduous. Upright, symmetrical trees bear heart-shaped to diamond-shaped leaves that turn rusty gold to brown in autumn. Growth habit and smooth trunks suggest birches. Use alders in Group Plantings and Multiple Trunk, Upright, and Slanting styles. Alders need plenty of moisture; set the container in a tray of water during the growing season. Prune in spring, summer.

Propagation: seeds.

BERBERIS THUNBERGII (Japanese barberry). Deciduous. This twiggy, spiny shrub adapts to a variety of styles other than Single Trunk. Slender, arching branches bear small, roundish leaves. Leaves are normally deep green, but the selection 'Atropurpurea' has bronze to purple-red leaves. Autumn color is yellow, orange, or bright red. Small yellow flowers in spring produce beadlike, bright red berries that remain on branches after leaf drop. Prune in winter, spring, and summer.

Propagation: seeds, semihardwood cuttings (with or without heels), ground and air layering.

Buxus microphylla sinica

BUXUS (boxwood). Evergreen (broad-leafed). These quintessential hedge plants make handsome bonsai specimens. Smooth wood can become thick and gnarly, a striking contrast to the small, oval leaves. Pinching and pruning will open up plants that tend to bear dense foliage. Use boxwood in Multiple Trunk, Windswept, Exposed Root, and Raft styles and also for Rock Plantings. Prune in spring, summer.

Propagation: softwood and semihardwood cuttings (heel cuttings work well).

Camellia sasanqua

CAMELLIA SASANQUA (Sasanqua). Evergreen (broad-leafed). Glossy oval leaves are an elegant accompaniment to white, pink, or red flowers that appear in autumn and early winter. Growth habit varies; some cultivars are compact and upright, others spreading and almost vinelike. Those with limber, willowy stems can be trained as Cascade, Windswept, and, with a little more effort, Weeping specimens. Typically, flowers will be a bit large for the size of the bonsai plant. Prune after flowering; new growth starts in late winter/early spring.

Propagation: semihardwood cuttings, ground and air layering.

CARPINUS (hornbeam). Deciduous. Fast growth and flexible stems make hornbeams easy to train as bonsai plants. Leaves are sawtooth-edged ovals that remain on plants well into autumn, turn yellow to rusty gold before dropping. The most common species are *C. betulus* (European hornbeam) and *C. caroliniana* (American hornbeam). Asian bonsai practitioners use various Chinese and Japanese species, including *C.*

eximia, C. japonica, C. laxiflora, and *C. turczaninovii.* Hornbeams are adaptable to a number of styles: Upright, Slanting, Multiple Trunk, Exposed Root, and Raft, as well as Group and Rock Plantings. Prune in winter, summer.

Propagation: seeds, semihardwood cuttings, air layering.

CASUARINA EQUISETIFOLIA (horsetail tree). Evergreen. At first glance, you might mistake this plant for a pine, but a closer look at the "needles" shows that they are long, slender, jointed green branches. Pendulous branches make this a good candidate for Weeping bonsai; you might also try it for Slanting and Cascade styles. Plant horsetail trees only in fairly mild-winter regions; they are hardy only to about 15°F/-9°C. Prune at any time.

Propagation: seeds, semihardwood cuttings.

CEDRUS (cedar). Evergreen (needle-leafed). These stalwart skyline specimens, often used for massive lawn plantings, reduce well to bonsai work. Short needles come in tufted clusters; color varies from green to blue-green to nearly gray, depending on the species or cultivar. Stiff-needled *C. atlantica* (Atlas cedar) is widely used; 'Glauca' is popular for its silvery blue needles. Softer needles and more flexible branches distinguish *C. deodara* (deodar cedar).

Beautiful Cascade bonsai can be created with cedars; other appropriate styles include Upright, Slanting, Literati, and Multiple Trunk. Prune in spring.

Propagation: seeds, air layering.

Cedrus atlantica

CELTIS (hackberry). Deciduous. Hackberries are related to elms, displaying similar oval to lance-shaped leaves that turn yellow in autumn. Several North American species are available—*C. laevigata* (sugarberry), *C. occidentalis* (common hackberry), *C. reticulata* (western hackberry)—along with *C. sinensis* (Chinese hackberry) from eastern Asia. Other species hail from southern Europe and western Eurasia. Hackberries are among the handful of trees you can train Broom style. Prune in winter, spring, and summer.

Propagation: seeds.

CHAENOMELES (flowering quince). Deciduous. Flowering quinces make showy bonsai specimens, with bright blossoms adorning otherwise bare branches from late winter to early spring. About 2 inches across, flowers resemble single to partially double roses in white, shades of pink, orange, or red. Glossy green oval leaves are fairly small, turn rusty yellow in autumn. Plants are naturally irregular in growth, usually twiggy with angular branching. Try flowering quince in Multiple Trunk, Exposed Root, and Root over Rock styles. Prune after flowering.

Propagation: semihardwood heel cuttings, ground and air layering.

CHAMAECYPARIS (false cypress). Evergreen (needle-leafed). Two species—*C. obtusa* (Hinoki false cypress) and *C. pisifera* (Sawara false cypress)—and numerous named variants of both form a pool of fine bonsai material. In general, tiny scalelike leaves are held in branching, flattened planes; in many named selections, these flattened foliage sprays are carried horizontally, giving the plant a layered appearance.

Chaenomeles

Chamaecyparis obtusa 'Nana'

Several 'Filifera' selections of *C. pisifera* have threadlike twigs, while *C. p.* 'Plumosa' and *C. p.* 'Squarossa' feature small, soft needles in feathery branch sprays. Both species have dark green foliage, but needle colors in named selections include blue-green, gray-green, and yellow. Try false cypresses in Upright, Slanting, Literati, Group, Rock, and Root over Rock styles. Prune in spring, summer.

Propagation: seeds, softwood heel cuttings, ground and air layering.

COTONEASTER. Evergreen (broad-leafed) and deciduous. Plants range from upright and fountainlike shrubs and shrub-trees to spreading ground covers. All feature small white or pinkish flowers (like tiny single roses) in spring, red to orange pea-size berries in autumn. Deciduous types offer orange to red autumn foliage. Best bonsai plants are found among the small-leafed, low-growing species. Evergreens include *C. buxifolius*, *C. congestus*, *C. microphyllus*, and *C. salicifolius* 'Repens'. Among the deciduous types are *C. adpressus*, *C. apiculatus*, and *C. horizontalis*. Cotoneaster is suited to Multiple Trunk and Exposed Root styles and Root over Rock and other Rock Plantings. Prune in winter, spring, and summer.

Propagation: seeds, semihardwood heel cuttings, ground and air layering.

CRATAEGUS (hawthorn). Deciduous. Twiggy, thorny trees by nature, hawthorns make appealing bonsai with all-season interest. Clusters of tiny white or pink flowers decorate plants in spring; red fruits form in summer; and foliage turns yellow, orange, or red in autumn, then drops to reveal branch structure in winter. Most species have lobed leaves; *C. crus-galli* and *C.* x *lavallei* have oval leaves with toothed margins. Use hawthorns for Multiple Trunk and Exposed Root styles and Group and Root over Rock plantings. Prune in winter, summer.

Propagation: seeds.

CRYPTOMERIA JAPONICA **(Japanese cedar, sugi).** Evergreen (needle-leafed). This Japanese timber tree has produced several dwarf variants suitable for bonsai work; the most widely available is *C. j.* 'Elegans', sometimes called plume cedar. Needlelike, soft-textured leaves to 1 inch in length densely clothe branches. Grayish green during the growing season, they change to coppery purple in cold weather. Train Japanese cedar in Upright, Slanting, and Literati styles; plants also make good Group Plantings. Dense growth will need periodic pinching and pruning; do this at any time.

Propagation: softwood heel cuttings, ground and air layering.

Cotoneaster microphyllus

Euonymus alata

EUONYMUS. Deciduous. Four species offer vivid, reddish pink color in autumn plus a display of orange to red, usually squarish fruits that open to reveal orange seeds. Corky ridges on stems distinguish *E. alata* (winged euonymus) from smooth-stemmed *E. europaea* (European spindle bush), *E. americana* (strawberry bush), and *E. atropurpurea* (wahoo). Capitalize on the naturally angular growth by training euonymus in Multiple Trunk styles as well as Slanting, Windswept, and Root over Rock designs. Prune during the dormant period.

Propagation: seeds, semihardwood cuttings.

FAGUS (beech). Deciduous. With their massive trunks and domed canopies, beeches possess an air of majesty and are often choices for park plantings. As bonsai, they offer sturdy, smooth-barked trunks and fairly symmetrical branching. Leaves turn brown in autumn, remain on stems well into winter. The most common species is *F. sylvatica* (European beech). Many named selections are available, including those with bronze and purple foliage, deeply cut leaves, and weeping branches. Less widely available are *F. grandifolia* (American beech) and *F. crenata* (Japanese beech). Beeches are best trained in Upright and Slanting styles; they also make effective Group Plantings. Prune in late winter, summer. Wire carefully: wood is brittle.

Propagation: seeds; grafting for named selections of European beech.

Ginkgo biloba

FRAXINUS (ash). Deciduous. Because of their rapid growth, ashes are good plants for the bonsai novice. Foliage consists of oval leaflets that generally turn brilliant yellow in autumn. Their naturally upright growth makes them good candidates for Upright styles and Group Plantings. Wire with care: branches are brittle. Prune in winter, summer.

Propagation: seeds.

GINKGO BILOBA (maidenhair tree). Deciduous. Bright green leaves have the shape of a scalloped fan— just the shape of a maidenhair fern leaflet. Spectacular autumn color is a bright butter yellow to gold. Naturally upright habit suggests training in Upright styles. Ability to sprout from the base also makes ginkgo a good candidate for Clump training. Prune in winter, summer.

Propagation: seeds, semihardwood and hardwood cuttings.

ILEX (holly). Evergreen (broad-leafed) and deciduous. The red berries of these plants are part of the winter holiday scene, but in bonsai hollies are primarily grown for foliage. And hollies with large, spiny foliage are less favored than those with small leaves, spiny or

plain. The majority of holly species bear female and male flowers on separate plants; a nearby male plant is needed for the female to produce berries.

Among evergreen species, *I. crenata* (Japanese holly) has small leaves that resemble boxwood (*Buxus*); *I. vomitoria* (yaupon) also has boxlike foliage and will produce red berries without a pollinator nearby. Deciduous *I. serrata* bears slightly larger, narrower, thin-textured leaves that color well before falling. These hollies make good Multiple Trunk specimens. Also try them for Upright styles and Group Plantings. Prune in spring, summer.

Propagation: semihardwood cuttings.

JUNIPERUS (juniper). Evergreen (needle-leafed). Junipers are virtually the perfect bonsai plants. They're tough, malleable, long-lived, and fine-textured. Good specimens can originate from cuttings; but some of the most beautiful examples of bonsai art are gnarled, old junipers collected from the wild. Age—or the appearance of it—suits these plants; *jin* and *shari* (see pages 74 and 75) seem to be natural components of mature specimens.

Almost any juniper is amenable to bonsai training. With more than 60 species plus countless named selections, you have a vast pool of material from which to choose. Some are naturally upright and treelike; others are shrub and ground cover plants. Junipers have two kinds of foliage: juvenile leaves are short, prickly needles, while mature foliage consists of tiny overlapping scales. Junipers can be trained in all styles except Broom. Prune at any time, though spring and summer are best. Don't cut back into leafless wood, or new growth may not occur.

Propagation: softwood and semihardwood cuttings, ground and air layering.

Juniperus chinensis

Malus sargentii

LAGERSTROEMIA INDICA (crape myrtle).
Deciduous. Bark is a special feature—smooth and gray, flaking to reveal pink patches beneath. During summer, plants may bear clusters of papery white, pink, red, or purple flowers. Small oval leaves become incandescent orange-red in autumn. Crape myrtle adapts to a variety of styles: Upright, Slanting, Multiple Trunk, Broom, Root over Rock. Prune in winter.

Propagation: seeds, semihardwood and hardwood cuttings.

LARIX (larch).
Deciduous. Larches are among the few needle-leafed plants that lose their foliage each autumn (see also *Metasequoia* and *Taxodium*). A fresh, apple-green new growth in spring matures to needles about 1 inch in length, which turn gold or russet in autumn. Natural growth is rigidly upright, making larches good for Upright styles and Group Plantings. You can also try training in Slanting and Literati styles. Most species prefer cool summer/chilly winter climates; *L. kaempferi* (Japanese larch) is more tolerant of warm, mild conditions. Prune in winter, summer; new growth will sprout from cuts made into leafless stems.

Propagation: seeds.

LIQUIDAMBAR STYRACIFLUA (American sweet gum).
Deciduous. From its 5-lobed leaves, you might mistake this tree for a maple, and the vivid colors of its autumn foliage reinforce that similarity. American sweet gum is a tall, fairly slender tree. Use it for Upright styles and Group Plantings. Because it will sprout from the base, you can also create Multiple Trunk specimens. Other styles to try are Raft and Root over Rock. Prune in winter, summer.

Propagation: seeds, softwood cuttings, air layering.

MALUS (crabapple).
Deciduous. These miniaturized apples present the maximum seasonal change. Springtime brings a floral display; autumn offers yellowish foliage; and small fruits decorate the branches from late summer into winter. Numerous species and named selections are available, but two stand out for bonsai work. Japanese flowering crabapple, *M. floribunda*, has white blossoms opening from red to pink buds; small fruits are yellow and red. Sargent crabapple, *M. sargentii*, is white-flowered (pink in the form 'Rosea') with tiny red fruits. Crabapples are suited to a variety of styles, including Informal Upright, Slanting, Multiple Trunk, and Root over Rock. Prune in winter, summer.

Propagation: seeds.

METASEQUOIA GLYPTOSTROBOIDES (dawn redwood).
Deciduous. Short needles and upright growth suggest *Sequoia sempervirens* (coast redwood), but these trees lose their needles in autumn in a glow of bronzy-brown. New spring foliage is light green. Dawn redwood is a natural for Group Plantings and also appropriate for Upright, Slanting, and Literati styles. Prune in winter, summer.

Propagation: seeds.

Liquidambar styraciflua

NANDINA DOMESTICA (heavenly bamboo).
Evergreen (broad-leafed). Upright stems and narrow leaflets present a bamboolike appearance, but this shrub is closely related instead to the barberries (*Berberis*). Foliage emerges pink to red in spring; turns pinkish gold, red, or maroon in autumn; and remains colorful during winter. Small-growing selections with reduced leaf and plant sizes are best for bonsai work. These include 'Compacta', 'Filamentosa', 'Harbour Dwarf', 'Nana', and 'Pygmaea'. Because plants naturally form clumps, heavenly bamboo is well adapted to Multiple Trunk styles. Stems are unbranched unless pruned; when pruned, two branches usually grow from beneath the cut. Prune in winter, summer.

Propagation: semihardwood cuttings.

OLEA EUROPAEA (olive). Evergreen (broad-leafed). Where winters are mild (lows above 15°F/-9°C) and summers fairly dry, you can create effective bonsai with olive. Plants have smooth gray bark, narrow leaves with silvery undersides. Their natural tendency is to grow a number of trunks, making them suitable for training in Multiple Trunk styles. Prune at any time; new growth sprouts freely from the base, so remove all unwanted shoots as they appear.

Propagation: seeds, semihardwood cuttings, ground and air layering.

PICEA (spruce). Evergreen (needle-leafed). Like many members of the pine family, spruces have upright trunks, tiers of regularly spaced branches, and a conical shape. Short needles densely cover branches, spiraling around them in bottlebrush fashion. Most species come from high latitudes or high altitudes, making them poor subjects for regions where winters are mild and summers are warm to hot.

Nandina domestica

Picea jezoensis

Several spruces are suitable for bonsai work, but it's no accident that the species most widely used is native to Japan: Yeddo spruce, *P. jezoensis*, has green and silver needles that remain under 1 inch in length; its variant, *P. j. hondoensis*, has even shorter needles and a more compact growth habit. The light green tufts of new growth in spring are as decorative as any floral display. Bonsai specialists may offer named selections with variations in needle color or size. Another spruce suited to bonsai training is *P. glauca* 'Conica' (dwarf Alberta spruce). This slow-growing, compact pyramid has ¾-inch-long needles that put on a "flowery" show of new growth similar to that of the Yeddo spruce.

Their upright symmetry makes spruces natural candidates for Upright styles and Group Plantings. But they also look good in Root over Rock and Clinging to Rock styles. Prune in spring; don't cut back to leafless branches, as new growth won't arise there.

Propagation: seeds, air layering.

PINUS (pine). Evergreen (needle-leafed). Pines are one of the classic bonsai plants. Though native to a wide range of climates and locales, they are also associated with the trying natural conditions that produce weather-ravaged plants that serve as models for several bonsai styles. Pines can be trained in Formal and Informal Upright, Slanting, Literati, Windswept, and Multiple Trunk styles. They're also suitable for Group and Root over Rock plantings; even Cascade style is not out of the question.

You can train practically any pine as bonsai, but the most effective specimens usually are created from species with shorter needles. Japanese black pine, *P. thunbergiana* (often sold as *P. thunbergii*), and Japanese white pine, *P. parviflora*, are favorite species. Other pines to try include mugho pine, *P. mugo mugo* (select plants with short needles), and Scots pine, *P. sylvestris*. In the Pacific Coast region, native species *P. balfouriana* (foxtail pine) and *P. contorta* (shore pine) can be used. In the Southwest, try several piñon pines: *P. cembroides*, *P. edulis*, and *P. monophylla*. In cold-winter northern and eastern regions, *P. banksiana* (jack pine) may be a good choice.

Potentilla fruticosa

Pinus parviflora

New growth in spring appears as "candles" at the tip of each branch. For greatest size increase, leave the candles alone. To restrict growth, cut them back to points of origin; several new candles will sprout from those points later that year or the following year. To simply limit growth, cut candles back part way; new growth will sprout from just beneath the cut. Cut candles before needles start to elongate. Prune branches in autumn when sap bleeding will be at a minimum. Some bonsai growers apply grafting wax to branch cuts to check bleeding. Don't cut back into bare wood, or no new growth will sprout.

Propagation: seeds, air layering.

POTENTILLA FRUTICOSA (potentilla, bush cinquefoil). Deciduous. These twiggy plants with attractive shredding bark and leaves composed of tiny leaflets make good bonsai choices. As a bonus, inch-wide blossoms resembling single roses in shades of yellow, white, or orange-red decorate plants during the summer. Autumn foliage is rusty yellow. Nurseries offer numerous named selections. Potentillas are suited to Multiple Trunk styles; you can also try them in Exposed Root and Root over Rock as well as other Rock Plantings. Prune in winter, spring, and summer.

Propagation: softwood cuttings, ground and air layering.

PRUNUS (apricot, cherry, plum). Deciduous. Flowers—and, to a lesser extent, fruits—are special features of all deciduous *Prunus* species. Bonsai favorites include several species from Japan. Earliest to flower (mid- to late winter) is *P. mume* (Japanese flowering apricot). Small, single pink blossoms later produce yellow fruits up to 1 inch in diameter. This is perhaps the longest-lived *Prunus* species; it becomes picturesque and gnarled with age.

Blazing orange to red foliage is an autumn feature of *P. sargentii* (Sargent cherry); spring flowers are blush pink, displayed against chestnut-colored bark. Larger blossoms—single, semi-double, or double—characterize the many selections of *P. serrulata* (Japanese flowering cherry). Colors include white and pink shades; double-flowered selections bear no fruits. From western Asia comes *P. cerasifera* (myrobalan or cherry plum); small white blossoms are followed by cherry-size red fruits.

These *Prunus* species are best used in styles that emphasize or accommodate irregularity: Slanting, Windswept, Multiple Trunk, Exposed Root, and Root over Rock. Prune after flowering, late summer.

Propagation: seeds, air layering.

PUNICA GRANATUM **(pomegranate).**
Deciduous. Colorful pomegranates offer bonsai possibilities, particularly in milder regions where winter temperatures remain above 10°F/-12°C. Bronzy new growth matures to glossy, bright green, narrow leaves; in autumn, foliage turns yellow before dropping. Small-growing selections are best for bonsai. These include 'Chico', with red-orange blossoms that look like carnations, and 'Nana', with single orange flowers followed by small, dull red fruits. Multiple Trunk styles are easiest with pomegranate, but you might also try Root over Rock and Exposed Root. Prune in winter.

Propagation: semihardwood cuttings.

Punica granatum

PYRACANTHA (firethorn). Evergreen. With naturally angular growth, firethorns easily become picturesque bonsai specimens. Narrow, dark green leaves appear on stems with needlelike thorns. Clusters of tiny white blossoms in spring produce pea-size fruits that mature in autumn to orange or red. Firethorn's growth habit suggests training in irregular styles— Slanting, Windswept, even Cascade. Others to try are Multiple Trunk, Exposed Root, and Root over Rock. Prune in winter, summer.

Propagation: seeds, semihardwood cuttings, ground and air layering.

PYRUS (pear). Deciduous. The familiar fruiting pear is simply the best known of a larger group of trees that offers good structure, white spring blossoms, and dazzling displays of autumn foliage color. The fruits they bear are small and unimportant.

A conical shape with horizontal limbs characterizes *P. calleryana* (Callery pear). Early spring flowers appear before foliage emerges; the glossy, leathery, broadly oval leaves turn to shades of brilliant purple-tinted red in autumn. In *P. pyrifolia* (Japanese sand pear), flowers and leaves may appear simultaneously on a tree of more upright habit. Leaves are longer and narrower than the Callery pear but take on the same colors in autumn. Both pears may be trained in Upright and Slanting styles as well as Multiple Trunk and Root over Rock plantings. Prune in winter, summer.

Propagation: seeds, air layering.

QUERCUS (oak). Evergreen and deciduous (both broad-leafed). Mighty oaks make mighty fine bonsai; their heavy trunks and gnarled branches suggest majesty on a small scale. The best species to use are those that bear relatively small leaves. Among evergreens, these include *Q. agrifolia* (coast live oak) and many other California and Oregon natives, *Q. coccifera* (kermes oak), *Q. ilex* (holly or holm oak), *Q. suber* (cork oak), and *Q. virginiana* (southern live oak). Choices are more limited among deciduous species: *Q. lobata* (valley oak) and *Q. robur* (English oak) have leaves in the 3- to 4-inch range. Oaks lend themselves to Informal Upright and Multiple Trunk styles. They also make attractive Root over Rock specimens. Prune in winter, summer.

Propagation: seeds.

Quercus agrifolia

Rhododendron (Satsuki azalea)

RHODODENDRON (azalea). Evergreen
(broad-leafed). Azaleas are easy to train, growing freely and sprouting new growth anywhere you make a cut. Older plants develop thick, gnarled trunks and major branches. And you get a blossom display in the bargain. Proportion is the chief concern: you want plants that have small leaves and flowers. This can be a problem, since most azaleas have been developed for large, showy blossoms. The best bonsai candidates are found among the Kurume and Satsuki hybrids. A visit to a nursery specializing in rhododendrons and azaleas may reveal other small-foliage species worth trying.

Informal Upright and Multiple Trunk are two styles to which azaleas adapt easily. Also try Exposed Root and Root over Rock. With careful training, even Broom style is possible. Prune in spring, summer.

Propagation: semihardwood cuttings, ground and air layering.

SEQUOIA SEMPERVIRENS (coast redwood).
Evergreen (needle-leafed). Strong, ramrod-straight trunks are covered in cinnamon-colored, shredding bark. Leaves appear almost delicate in contrast: narrow and needlelike, carried in flattened sprays, they emerge bright light green in spring and darken as they mature. Upright trunk and relatively narrow branch spread make this a good choice for Formal Upright training and Group and Raft plantings. Cut to the ground, a plant will send up a number of shoots that you can select for Multiple Trunk training. Specimens with *jin*-trained apexes (see page 74) give the impression of lightning-struck forest patriarchs. Prune in spring; new growth will sprout from leafless branches.

Propagation: seeds, semihardwood cuttings.

SEQUOIADENDRON GIGANTEUM (giant
sequoia). Evergreen (needle-leafed). Trunk and bark suggest its relative the coast redwood (preceding), but foliage immediately sets it apart. Giant sequoia leaves are short, overlapping, needle-pointed scales that look much like the juvenile foliage of junipers. Growth is dense and rigidly upright, forming a solid green cone. Formal Upright and Group Plantings are the best bonsai treatments. Prune in spring.

Propagation: seeds.

SERISSA FOETIDA. Evergreen (broad-leafed).
This lovely small shrub deserves a common name that would reflect its delicacy and refinement. A profusion of glossy, tiny leaves (about ¼ to ½ inch long) clothe a densely branched, somewhat angular plant. Small, funnel-shaped blossoms are scattered over this backdrop from spring to autumn; they can be white or pink, single- or double-flowered, and have green or variegated leaves. With its rather angular branching habit, serissa adapts to such styles as Slanting and Windswept; you also can train it in Double Trunk, Triple Trunk, and Raft styles, as well as Root over Rock plantings. Plants are suited to regions where winter temperatures remain above 20°F/-7°C. Prune in spring, summer.

Propagation: softwood and semihardwood cuttings.

Serissa foetida

Taxodium distichum

TAXODIUM DISTICHUM (bald cypress).
Deciduous. In general appearance, this tree suggests a softer-textured, smoother-barked *Sequoia sempervirens* (coast redwood). Sturdy, upright trunks contrast with the feathery appearance of light green, needlelike leaves carried in flattened sprays. But unlike its redwood relative, these needles turn rusty brown in autumn and drop, leaving a bare winter silhouette.

Use bald cypress for Formal Upright and Group bonsai. The closely related *T. mucronatum* (Montezuma cypress) has a strongly weeping branch habit; try it as a Weeping bonsai. In warm-winter climates, its leaves may remain evergreen. Both species thrive on plenty of water; potted specimens can stand in shallow pans of water throughout the growing season. Prune in spring.

Propagation: seeds, semihardwood cuttings.

TILIA (linden—"lime" in Europe). Deciduous.
Lindens are large, dense trees of broadly conical shape covered in irregularly heart-shaped leaves. Though all can be used for bonsai, those with smaller foliage are best. *T. cordata* (little-leaf linden) has the smallest leaves: to 3 inches long and broad, dark green with paler undersides. Its hybrid *T.* x *euchlora* (Crimean linden) is similar but has slightly larger leaves. Both feature yellow autumn color. Use lindens for Upright, Slanting, and Multiple Trunk styles. Prune in winter, summer.

Propagation: seeds, air layering.

TSUGA (hemlock). Evergreen (needle-leafed).
Though they grow as upright cones of foliage, hemlocks are inherently graceful. Soft needles (under 1 inch) grow densely on arching to drooping branchlets. All hemlocks need humidity for good growth; some prefer coolness, while others tolerate some heat. Best species for cool-summer regions of the Pacific Coast is *T. heterophylla* (western hemlock). For warmer summer temperatures in the northeastern and mid-Atlantic states, *T. canadensis* (Canada hemlock), *T. caroliniana* (Carolina hemlock), and *T. sieboldii* (Japanese hemlock) are the best choices. Use hemlocks in Formal and Informal Upright, Slanting, Literati, and Multiple Trunk styles and as Group Plantings. Prune in spring, summer; new growth will sprout if you cut back to bare wood.

Propagation: seeds, air layering.

ULMUS PARVIFOLIA (Chinese elm).
Deciduous. Of the numerous elm species, the Chinese elm is perhaps the best for bonsai work. It's a fast grower with limber branches that bear oval leaves to 2 inches long. In mild winters, foliage is partially to totally evergreen. Especially favored for bonsai are smaller-leafed selections such as 'Catlin', 'Seiju', and 'Hokkaido'; the latter two have leaves to ¼ inch long and bark that becomes corky with age. Multiple Trunk and Broom styles take advantage of the plant's natural growth habit. Prune in winter, spring.

Propagation: seeds, ground and air layering for named selections.

Tsuga heterophylla

Ulmus parvifolia 'Catlin'

VIBURNUM. Deciduous and evergreen (broad-leafed). Best known as background and specimen shrubs, viburnums include the familiar "snowball bushes" *V. macrocephalum macrocephalum* and *V. opulus* 'Roseum'. Though bulky plants by nature, some viburnums reduce well to bonsai size.

Deciduous *V. plicatum tomentosum* (doublefile viburnum) becomes a broadly spreading shrub with a horizontal branch pattern. Clusters of white flowers appear along tops of branches in midspring, carried above the oval leaves that color purplish red in autumn.

Evergreen *V. tinus* (laurustinus) is a dense, upright plant with leathery oval leaves; new stems are wine red. Small white flowers during winter are followed by metallic blue berries. Plants are semi-tender, hardy to about 0°F/-18°C.

Both viburnums are good in Multiple Trunk styles; doublefile viburnum, with its wide-spreading branches, also is a candidate for Informal Upright and Slanting training. Prune in winter, summer.

Propagation: softwood and semihardwood cuttings, ground and air layering.

WISTERIA. Deciduous. Wisteria's glory is its spring display of sweet pea–like blossoms in long, pendent clusters. These inevitably are out of proportion to the bonsai plant, but the show is so spectacular that you easily forgive the temporary incongruity. Foliage is quite lush and large, consisting of numerous oval to lance-shaped leaflets per leaf. Because of leaf size, wisteria is best grown as medium or large specimens.

The most common species, *W. sinensis* (Chinese wisteria), has foot-long clusters of flowers on bare wood. Both *W. floribunda* (Japanese wisteria), with the longest floral clusters, and *W. venusta* (silky wisteria), with the shortest, blossom after leaves have emerged. Grow wisteria in styles that show off the flowers: Slanting, Cascade, Windswept, Weeping, and Multiple Trunk, if you allow for a wide branch spread. Prune in winter, spring, and summer. Plants are vigorous vines that need regular pinching and pruning to stay within bounds.

Propagation: air layering; plants raised from seeds take many years to flower.

ZELKOVA SERRATA **(sawleaf or Japanese zelkova).** Deciduous. The natural growth habit of sawleaf zelkova is in the form of a broom—many branches splaying upward and outward from nearly the same point atop the trunk. Naturally, this is a favorite for the Broom style of bonsai. Its overall appearance suggests an elm but with beechlike smooth, gray bark that becomes flaky in old specimens. The 2- to 3-inch oval, serrated leaves turn yellow, red, or reddish brown in autumn. Prune in winter, summer.

Propagation: seeds, air layering.

Zelkova serrata

INDEX